Ashly

Amish Confidential

Amish Confidential:

The Bishop's Son Shatters The Silence

Chris Burkholder

Argyle Publishing

Amish Confidential
Copyright © 2006 Chris Burkholder
Argyle Publishing

All rights reserved. No part of this book may be reproduced (except for inclusion in reviews), disseminated or utilized in any form or by any means, electronic or mechanical, including photocopying, recording, or in any information storage and retrieval system, or the Internet/World Wide Web without written permission from the author or publisher.

Though this is a true story, and the events told in this story are entirely my own, to respect confidentiality, and to protect and respect the identities of the innocent and victims alike, all the names have been changed.

For more information about this title please contact:
Argyle Publishing
P.O. Box 72 • Argyle, Iowa • 52619
www.argylepublishing.org

Book design by:
Arbor Books
www.arborbooks.com

Printed in United States

Library of Congress Control Number: 2005908120
ISBN: 0-9772680-0-4

To my wife and children whom I love dearly. Walk in the truth both earthly and spiritually so that your days may be filled with blessings from our Heavenly Father. Do not doubt or be afraid of the truth. Where there is truth, there is also faith and freedom. May the Lord bless you each and every day of your life.

A Message from Chris Burkholder

I believe that the God-given right to freedom, respect and dignity will be neither gained nor enjoyed until the truth is uncovered and confronted. Truth, the pulse of life, is our association with certainty. It is faith, belief and conviction, unadulterated. Truth is authenticity. Therefore, I am committed to bringing my truth into the light, with all its colors and nuances. Writing my book was at times mentally and emotionally agonizing, but life comes forth in pain. However, the joy of holding a new born shadows any memory of physical distress.

My book is a "new born" testament to the power of truth. I wrote it neither to seek revenge nor point an accusatory finger. Instead, it is my intention to speak out against the foes of truth, the hypocrisy and lies that shackle and destroy, making unwilling victims of innocent individuals, unaware that pain and humiliation are not an integral part of an acceptable daily life.

Truth is an influential and potent force, undefeatable and unchanging. It is also the key to finding personal satisfaction, self-respect, dignity and peace of mind.

"And the word was made flesh, and dwelt among us. And we saw His glory-glory as of the only begotten son-full of grace and of truth!"

–John 1:14

May God bless you as He has blessed us, and if you ask Him, humbly and in good faith, He will, for the Lord is the Way, the Life and the Truth.

–Chris and Shannon Burkholder

I

Bowling Green, Missouri

Summer of 1978–
Fall of 1979

CHAPTER 1

The twelve hour work day was endless, and to a six year old boy born in Bowling Green, Missouri, it was unbearable during the summer months. The sun burned through my crisp white shirt searing my shoulders as I worked outdoors. They already ached from the weight of the wide suspenders I wore to keep my oversized pants from falling down. In keeping with the Amish tradition, Mom made my pants from coarse material. They were heavy and stiff causing me to perspire profusely. Once soaked with sweat they hugged my thighs and calves, irritating my skin. With every step I took big red welts formed on my legs, itching and burning as I went about doing my chores. By the day's end I was in misery.

Much as I looked forward to the twilight, the Elders welcomed every sunrise as a gift from the Lord: A Lord who in return expected obedience, respect and a hard day's work from man, woman and child.

It was shortly after sundown and chores were completed. Mom and Dad took me, my brother and sisters over to Grandpa Burkholder's to spend the night. It was the summer of 1978.

I was the third child and first son born on September 27, 1972 to David Burkholder and Amelia Kemp. Amish couples were prolific and almost every year Mom and Dad added a new addition to the family, until eleven children had been born.

I remember the day my parents were invited to a wedding quite distant from our farm house. They had made arrangements with an outsider, the 'English man,' to take them in his van. The Amish considered anyone who was not part of the tradition as 'English.'

In the Old Order Amish Community in which I was born and raised, the sole means of transportation was a black horse-drawn buggy. If for whatever reason an Amish person had to travel a long distance he would turn to the 'English' for transportation. They were 'modern' folks, who drove gasoline-powered vehicles.

My grandpa, Herman Burkholder was a Preacher and religious fanatic who helped Dad in Church on Sundays. Grandpa was a giant to me; a big intimidating man with a towering presence. He stood six feet tall and weighed over two hundred pounds. A sickening odor betrayed his presence. When he came close the stench of his sweat-drenched shirt was unbearable. It was, however, a testament of his diligence to farm life. He was unattractive with deep linear lines crossing his cheeks and forehead in bold crosses. His sixteen inch white beard and matted hair gave him a dramatic look. His complexion was ruddy and weather-beaten and the yellow wide-brimmed straw hat he wore from dawn to dusk did little to protect his skin from the sun. The impassive blue eyes never smiled. I was frightened of Grandpa.

Grandpa's self-possessed gaze was characteristic of a man who firmly believed he knew it all. His ignorance, abusive behavior and two–faced personality were neither acknowledged nor accepted as part of who he was. Not by him that is.

When we arrived at Grandpa's he was in the barn tending to his chores. His farm was about a mile and a half from ours. We were greeted at the front door, by Grandma, a squat lady with a contagious laugh who had gained my affection early on because she was generous in giving out candy. She was clever and knew eating the candy kept us busy and quiet. This evening would be no exception.

"Christy, come over here to Grandma and let me check your nails," she said. Everyone in my family called me Christy.

"OK Grandma," I said, excited, knowing what was about to

happen. I walked over to her with my hands open palms down, eager to taste the sweetness of her chewy treats. I could clearly hear the crunching sound of my teeth grinding the shiny sassafras morsels into powder. Sassafras is a sweet glassy candy made from boiled down corn syrup and water.

Suddenly the door creaked. It was an old, battered wooden door that had been screened to keep the mosquitoes from entering. I turned to see Grandpa come into the house.

"Good evening," he said with an expressionless face. "I see the children have arrived." He handed his straw hat to Grandma, quickly glanced at the long, rectangular oak table and went over to the basin to wash up. Although it was 1978, in the Amish community modern conveniences were shunned. Neither electricity nor sophisticated appliances were permitted. Grandpa's nightly ritual of going over to the pitcher-pump and pumping water into a basin was a silent signal for Grandma to prepare supper. He was hungry and tired, and found comfort in the aroma of seared meat, roasted corn and fresh baked bread. Mixed with the scent of oil from the gas lanterns these familiar aromas offered him a special evening pleasure. When everyone was seated around the table, Grandma put my one year old brother William in his little chair. William Burkholder, born January 20, 1976, was Mom and Dad's fifth child.

"William, sit still for a moment while I get supper ready," Grandma said. She walked back to the small counter next to the cook stove, which served as an oven, grill and burner and took out the cold packed hamburger meat for the evening meal. The beef was carved from the carcass of a slaughtered cow days ago and had been passed through her wood handle grinder. Once finely chopped it was preserved in glass jars.

Grandma overturned the jar and emptied its contents. She sliced the meat about an inch thick, fried it, and smothered it in ketchup and mustard. It was served with a piece of sautéed tongue and fried brains. Water and warm cow's milk were served with the meal. The room was dimly lit by a gas lantern hanging from a hook directly over the table and created a serene atmosphere.

William was still crying and fussing and carrying on non stop. His energy seemed limitless: He was a typical one year old.

"William, my sweet boy, it's time for supper: Why all the fussing?" Grandma said, caressing his silky blond hair.

"There's no need for crying," she continued, trying to quiet him.

"Be quiet, William," Grandpa said, with little compassion for the small child who continued to wail. William's language was laughter and tears; his words chuckles and sobs. However, Grandpa was too self-centered to take the time to understand.

"Let's bow our heads and ask the Lord's blessing for the food we are about to eat," he said, ignoring the ruckus. "We have been blessed and we need to give thanks."

After the Amen, Grandpa placed a fair helping of food on William's plate before serving himself. The child was cranky, without appetite and refused to eat. Grandpa was tired, edgy and intolerant.

"Now William shut up and eat your supper," Grandpa said.

His patience had run out long before he came to the table. The sobbing continued. Grandpa leaned over across the table and delivered a swift slap across William's face with his calloused palm. I sat horrified, imagining his cold, bumpy hand meeting William's soft, delicate cheek. I was petrified. There was no escape from physical brutality: Not yet anyway.

The sharp, crackling sound of the slap echoed in the room. The pain interrupted the stunned boy's wails for a brief second. I held my breath. The room fell into silence. Grandpa, angry and upset, forced the small boy to pick up his fork and eat.

"William, I mean it, stop this nonsense. I've been milking cows and tossing hay all day. I'm tired and I'm hungry. I want to eat my supper in peace," he shouted.

His anger and frustration caused him to sweat. The foul odor spread throughout the room, overpowering the appetizing aroma of Grandma's meal.

William continued to protest, and turned away from his food. His tiny face was beet red from the slap. Once again Grandpa reached across the table. His clumsy movement tumbled a glass of water. Ignoring the mishap, he snatched the fork from William's hand and thrust it into the child's mouth.

"William, if you don't shut up and eat your supper, I'll shove it down your throat, piece by piece," Grandpa shouted. William began to choke and gag, gasping for air. Bits and pieces of fried meat fell from his quivering lips. The ketchup splattered from his plate on to the table, hitting him in the face. His hair and shirt were covered with thick red stains.

Furious, Grandpa pushed his chair across the wooden floor. It was unvarnished and splintered easily. The screech of Grandpa's chair digging into the wood hurt my ears. Grandpa jumped to his feet, grabbed William by the shoulders and yanked him out of the seat. The chair toppled over, crashing to the floor. It hit the brittle wood with a thud then rebounded from the force and slammed down again. Unconcerned by his surroundings, Grandpa carried the terrified child across the room. William was crying and kicking his legs frantically. Grandpa sat himself down, turned William over his knees and gave him three open hand floggings across his bottom. The child howled and screamed, blood rushing to his face. Grandma rose and made her way over to rescue William.

"Stay back! Sit down!" Grandpa shouted. "I'll handle the boy. It's time this reckless behavior stops. He's old enough to sit and eat like the rest of us. I won't tolerate this nonsense any longer."

William continued his tirade, bawling, sobbing and screeching: From pain, but more from fear and horror. Grandpa returned to the table and continued to eat his supper, making small talk with Grandma and acting as if nothing had occurred. The indifference was frightening that evening: A pattern was set.

After supper, I lay in bed unable to sleep. My thoughts turned to William and the mean way in which Grandpa treated him.

The following day when we returned home, my older sister Rebecca, who was nine at the time, told Mom and Dad Grandpa had slapped William across the face then flogged him three times. Rebecca Burkholder, born October 16, 1969, was Mom and Dad's first child.

"Dad," Rebecca said, excited, "Grandpa gave William a lashing on his bottom last night."

"Whatever for?" Mom asked. "Why would he do that? William's just a baby."

"'Cause he was fussing and didn't want to eat his supper," Rebecca said.

"Grandpa said he was tired and told William to shut up and eat, but William didn't listen. When Grandpa tried to stick the fork in his mouth, he turned his head, spilling food all over and Grandpa got real mad."

"That seems a bit harsh for a small child," Mom replied.

Listening to her words that evening, it seemed as if she were talking about domesticating a wild farm animal and not her one year old child.

My sister Rebecca was a slender girl with clear blue eyes and sleek sandy hair. Though often silent in her approach to life, she was bright and quick to learn. Unfortunately, she was not gifted with a sense of humor. Instead, she had a devious and manipulative personality and seemed dedicated to getting me in trouble. Her tattle-taling nature caused me many lashings.

After listening to Rebecca's story, it was Dad's turn to step in. Hearing the details of the event, he came to Grandpa's defense.

"We will not discuss this incident further," Dad told Mom. "I know Grandpa took those measures to teach William a lesson. The boy is old enough to learn some manners. We can't have him crying and carrying on every time we sit for supper. Supper is the time of day when the family gets together after a hard day's work, to enjoy a meal and talk about the day's events. I'll not hear any more about this. Do you understand, Amelia? And that goes for you also, Rebecca, not another word."

"Yes," Mom said, her gaze focused on her fingernails.

"OK, Dad," Rebecca replied.

What Grandpa did to William was frightening. Although it was the first time I witnessed his cruel and aggressive behavior, from that day on I began to despise him. Hearing my Dad's order to dismiss Grandpa's cruel actions only added to my distress. I was frustrated and upset. Both Grandpa and Dad's behavior was beginning to confuse me. I did not fully understand what was happening, but I knew I didn't like it one bit. A seed was planted.

Early one morning, several days later, Uncle Matthew, Uncle Ben and Grandpa came over to the farm house to visit with Dad. I heard the crackling of their steps and knew they were walking along the winding gravel path leading to the front porch.

Amish homes in Bowling Green, Missouri were of simple wood construction with metal roofs. Ours was no exception. Although white in color, time and the elements had weathered its façade, giving it a drab, grayish look. The house was not very large, just a story and a half. It was, however, much in need of a painting. Time was spent doing barn chores and attending Sunday service and little was left to take care of the house. Mom and my sisters kept it clean and tidy but Dad seldom, if ever, attended to the exterior. The windows were small and set high, just the right size for privacy.

The front porch was the main entrance. On the porch a rusted swing swayed in the wind. I had spent many days swinging, dreaming and listening to the swishing sound I made as I soared higher and higher. I can still hear the rhythmic squeaks of the rust-eaten chains swinging to and fro as I swiveled and swung. These chains anchored the seat to the ceiling and served as a guard against falling off. I held on to them as I swung, enjoying the safety they provided. Afterwards my tiny hands would be red and irritated and I would notice the imprint of the links on my palms.

The knotted porch floor was dry and brittle and creaked with every step I took. It led to an old wooden screen door. There were no steel jams and in the winter Mom would roll up a rug and jam it under the half inch space between the threshold and the door to keep the wind and snow from coming inside the house. I could still see her hunched over near the door ready to block out the elements.

My thoughts were interrupted by the sound of Uncle Matthew's gruff voice. "Morning," he said, as he pulled open the screen door. "Good morning. It's brutal out there today,"

Grandpa said while Uncle Ben appeared, sliding in beside the two men. He smiled and patted me on the head.

Uncle Matthew Burkholder was a middle-aged man with short black hair, brown eyes and an athletic build. He was light of complexion, almost ashen, and had an undersized face for a sturdy man and a pair of perfectly bowed legs. It was almost comical to watch him walk, especially when the wind betrayed his defect. It would pull his wide pants until they clung tightly around his legs. I remember giggling when I saw him pass by.

Uncle Ben Burkholder was part of the "young folk," a short blonde haired boy with a prominent mouth. He carried himself with his head tilted back; a position which accentuated his sly glance, giving him a shrewd look. When Uncle Ben laughed, it was in short, staccato gasps. I always thought he sounded more like an animal than a man.

That morning, I was excited by the arrival of my uncles and curious about the reason for their stopover. My eyes followed them as they headed towards the barn. I tagged along several paces behind, my short legs unable to keep up with their swiftness. I was eager to discover the reason for their visit.

My Dad, David Burkholder, called Davie by his friends and family, was born November 16, 1945. He was a strapping, heavy set man, with one hundred and ninety pounds distributed on a five foot five inch frame. His hair was black and sleek and his ten inch dark beard gave him a stern, dismal look. Dad was a Bishop in the community, the most powerful authority figure responsible for my religious upbringing. He instilled a fear of the Lord in his children and in his flock, but more importantly he taught me his word was the rule. He governed his family and his flock and his way was not to be contradicted. However, I soon learned, he did not always practice what he preached.

Dad, Uncle Ben and Uncle Matthew entered the barn and brought out a young horse. I held my breath and waited. Suddenly I heard Dad say; "Get back, Ben, before he gives you a good swift kick and knocks you to the ground." My interest peaked and though I was unaware of what was happening, I knew something thrilling was in the making. I could feel the rush of excitement in my gut.

Through the corner of his eye, Dad noticed me drawing close to the barn.

"Christy, go back to the house," he said "This is no place for a small boy. You can come back later to help me with the milking. Go on now, we have things to do, and you're holding us up." Reluctantly I obeyed. The Bishop did not tolerate disobedience. The Bible clearly says, "Honour thy father and thy mother," and I was told I needed to follow that commandment if I feared and shunned the ire of Dad.

Disappointed, I turned and left the barn. When I arrived at the house I noticed Mom was seated near the window directly under the sun's morning glare. Her head was bent and thrust forward. She appeared to be concentrating on something she was sewing. Perhaps she was quilting or making Dad a new pair of britches. She could also be making a cape for herself.

Amish women made all the clothes for their family, using a blend of materials that did not require much ironing. Clothes were somber, loose fitting and drab. Women wore simple one piece dresses in dark solid colors; black, purple, brown and charcoal. Aprons were pinned over the dresses with open straight pins since no buttons were permitted. Bonnets and shawls were worn when leaving the farm.

Men wore oversized, dark, heavy trousers held firm with suspenders. They were un-cuffed and creaseless. Their jackets were cut straight, designed without lapels and closed with hooks and eyes. Shirts were solid blue or white with long sleeves. Ties and sweaters were not worn. Since zippers were not allowed, pants were fastened with buttons. Any other way of dressing was considered mundane and not accepted in the community. The Old Order Amish believed in humility and in a distinctive separation from the outside world.

Mom, Amelia Kemp, born November 4, 1946 was an attractive, plump woman with warm dark eyes and straight black hair. Since Amish women did not cut their hair, Mom gathered it under her white linen prayer cap and knotted it in a tightly pulled bun. Married women wore white caps while girls and children wore black.

Amish men had beards and long hair but no moustaches. They covered their heads with wide brimmed hats, either felt or straw depending on the season.

Mom was a smart, diligent, family oriented mother of eleven children. Growing up I remember her sweet disposition, understanding ways and dedication to her family's needs. She was open, engaging and used words generously.

Since Mom was busy with her sewing, I made a speedy decision to sneak out and return to the barn, curious to see what Dad and my uncles were up to. I wondered what all the fuss was about and why I had not been allowed to stay. Quickly and as quietly as possible, I slipped through the shop and up the hay mow, just in time to catch Dad throw the horse to the ground. I heard a loud thump and my pulse quickened.

"Hurry, tie him up," Dad said breathlessly. He was not one to show much emotion. I saw Uncle Matthew reach out and grab a long leather strap. It was worn and cracked from overuse. He bound the horse's slender hind legs with four brisk turns of the strap. The horse kicked and protested. Dad kneeled over the prone animal and I noticed several drops of sweat pour down his face and settle on his beard. They seemed to glisten for a brief second before disappearing into the matted strands of hair. Dad steadied the horse's heaving abdomen with the firm steady hand of someone familiar with this procedure.

"I've cut through his sac," he said. "He's got thick skin, this colt." I heard a ripping sound as the knife cut through, removing his testicles. I watched in awe, fascinated. A splattering of bright red blood covered Dad's hands and clothes, and turned the hay a vivid crimson.

"Get me a towel, Ben," Dad said, "quick, this is a bloody mess!"

Ben searched and found a soiled rag. The men watched the blood squirt for a few moments. They looked proud and satisfied. I now understood why Dad had to do this and why he did not want me around. This was a man's job. Castrating a horse took guts. It was a big important event and I wanted to do it myself. I was impatient to learn and decided I would become skilled by watching and imitating the actions of others.

The following day, while helping Dad with the milking, I sat opposite him on the other side of the cow. Suddenly I noticed a Tom cat. He had his butt turned towards me while slurping some milk. His hanging testicles caught my attention and stirred my imagination. I thought about what I had seen yesterday in the barn and an idea popped into my head.

"Dad, I have to poop. I'm going to the out house," I said. "Do you want me to come back right away? Cause I really don't know how long it's gonna take."

Dad nodded his approval.

"Ate too much of Mom's shoofly pie, I see," Dad said. He rose from his stool and headed down to the milk house with the milk. I ran towards the shop, darting through the corn crib so as not to be seen or heard. My heart raced with the thrill of anticipation; I felt every throbbing beat as I headed towards a new adventure.

Once in the shop I spotted the castrating knife. It was the same one I had seen Dad use on the horse. The knife had a steel blade with a sharp hook on the end. I stuffed it into my pocket, gathered some twine from the shop, tightly wound it around my suspenders and went back to the barn just in time to help Dad milk another cow. After the milking, he returned a second time to the milk house to deposit the milk. I knew he had one more cow to milk so I glanced over my shoulder to check on Mom and my sisters. I was happy to see they were busy at the far end of the parlor completing their daily chores.

I turned and ran outside. I felt free to follow my calling, snatched the Tom cat and tucked him under my arm. I dashed to the back of the barn and out through the machine shed. Breathless, I headed down to the creek. It rippled and gurgled behind the hog house. The echoes were energizing.

The cat was docile and did not offer much resistance. I tied him up and, feeling a bit anxious, gently stroked his back.

"It's going to be OK," I said. "It'll be done in a minute. This is something I have to do. This is a big important job. I saw Dad do it so I know what I'm doing. It'll hurt a little bit, but I have to do it. I'll be gentle," I continued, thinking with my six year old brain that my words would make it less painful for him.

The vivid images of Dad and my uncles castrating the horse ran wild in my mind. I knew I could do it. I untangled the twine from around my suspenders and fastened the cat to the exposed roots of a tree stump. I grabbed one of his testicles with my free hand. It felt hard and soft at the same time and kept slipping out of my grasp. Grimacing, I sliced the sac open with one sharp jab of the knife. Thick scarlet blood squirted from the wound, drenching my fingers. The cat let out a hair-raising screech.

"Hold still," I said and tried to hold him steady. "It'll be over soon." He resisted, scratching me several times on the arm. I noticed my blood was lighter in color and more transparent than his. Determined to succeed, I tied him to the root once again and with a swift hard thrust I cut into him. "I've got to do this!" I told him. "Dad did it yesterday to the horse and he's OK." I said. "It'll be over in a minute, just hold steady."

In agony from my two merciless "incisions," the cat thrashed about until he broke free.

"Get back here!" I shouted. He scampered back up to the barn. Chasing after him I returned to the barn.

Dad was seated milking the third cow. Without removing his hands from the animal's udders he turned toward me.

"Christy, where have you been," he said "I've been waiting for you."

"It takes a long time to poop, Dad," I lied.

With the foolish security of a six year old, I was certain Dad believed my fib. I sat down to help him finish milking.

Dad and I continued the milking. The Tom cat came in for his usual drink of milk. His butt was turned towards Dad, placing the slashed and hanging testicle in full view.

Puzzled, Dad said, "what's the matter with the cat?"

"I don't know," I replied, lowering my gaze to my bare feet.

"What do you mean you don't know? Don't you see he has been cut and mutilated?" Dad said, upset.

"Listen, Christy, do you know anything about this? Do you have a knife in your pocket?" Dad asked, already knowing the answer.

"No," I lied. "Nothing's in my pocket, Dad."

"Get over here right now," Dad said. "We'll see what's in your pocket!"

I took a few steps forward. My stomach churned. With a brisk move Dad reached into my pocket and pulled out the knife. It was stained with fresh blood.

Realizing I was caught and fully aware of the consequences I began to sob; a standard but useless procedure which never brought positive results.

"I don't know how it got there," I wailed.

Dad was losing his patience. "Do you think you can just get by with a lie, Christy?" He said, "answer me when I ask you a question!"

"It's wrong to tell a lie, Christy. You do know that, don't you?" Dad said. "I want an answer from you right now!"

"Yes, Dad" I said cringing inside.

"Yes, what, Christy?" Dad raised his tone.

"Yes, it's wrong to lie, Dad," I said, knowing what was about to happen.

Dad grabbed one of the long sticks used to tame out of control cows.

"Stand up straight, Christy," he said. I obeyed. He flogged me several times across my butt. The reverberating whack of the stick lashing my bottom scared me, even though it would become a familiar sound throughout my childhood and boyhood.

"Christy, take the knife and put it on the table," Dad said after the beating. I did as I was told. I knew I had done wrong. The whipping made me feel better about stealing the knife and hurting the cat: Almost.

One Sunday morning the family was united for breakfast around a big old oak table in the kitchen. Behind the table, directly under the window, there was a bench where the children sat. Mom and Dad each had a chair. A gas lantern burning white gas hung from the ceiling on a big hook. It hovered above our heads as we ate. Another lamp was placed in the center of the table and one in the wash area. The fourth light was stuck in a lamp holder and set in front of a mirror. The reflection threw a glare into the room. The kitchen walls were unpainted white sheet rock, dreary and abrasive to the touch. I noticed Mom was at the cook stove getting ready to serve breakfast.

My baby brother William was still teething and it was obvious by his crying and fussing that he was in a lot of pain. Dad was exasperated because the baby would not calm down. He rose abruptly from his seat at the head of the table and snatched William from Mom's arms. As was common procedure for him, he grabbed a spoon from the table and jammed it into William's mouth, splitting open the gum where the tooth was buried. Blood gushed from the open cut running down the baby's mouth and onto the front of his shirt. The rush of this warm red liquid scared William. He screamed and gagged. He was terrified of Dad and of the excruciating pain the man had caused him. With blood-stained hands Dad gave the howling child back to Mom. I watched in tears, fearful of the blood William was losing and upset by Dad's brutality. I looked at him with a distant, questioning expression. I did not yet fully understand who Dad was, but I already knew I did not like what he did.

As a young boy with a vivid imagination, wild ideas popped into my head. One day I stood watching the chickens strut about waddling their butts and making loud clucking sounds. I was not able to resist temptation and snatched one from the nest. I tucked her under my arm and ran behind the hog house and down to the corn field. It was mid June and the corn was about knee high. I decided it would be fun to set the chicken free among the tall husks and watch her scamper about. I grabbed a stick and darted in and out of the corn rows chasing after her. Breathless and laughing I caught and killed her. Once lifeless I took her down to the creek and covered her with dried leaves. I felt guilty about what I had done but the exhilaration far outweighed the responsibility.

I went back and killed two other chickens. The thrill was overwhelming, yet in my gut I felt I was in trouble. I knew I had better get rid of the evidence, quick. I ran back down to the creek, dug a hole, buried the chickens and covered them with broken twigs and leaves. I was certain I would get away with it. Most probably Fritz would be blamed.

Fritz was a black and white mutt with a restless nature who resembled a German Shepherd. He was a farm dog and mingled with the other animals without usually causing too much trouble. Being skittish and curious, however, I knew he would sniff out the chickens, dig them up, carry them up to the barn and eat them. And so it was.

The following day, at milking time, Dad noticed Fritz approaching, dragging one of the chickens. He was already famous for stealing eggs so there was no questioning this time. Dad pulled Fritz over and wound a piece of twine around his neck to hold him steady. He then beat him with a stick for killing the chickens. Listening to the poor dog's howls and whimpers, I felt sad knowing full well Fritz didn't do it. He gained the reputation of a chicken killer because of my actions. I knew that one more incident of naughty behavior would be a death sentence for Fritz. I was right.

CHAPTER 2

The Lord's Prayer was a daily plea for help. It was often invoked because life even for a small child was full of temptations and falling into temptation led to severe and painful whippings. Every morning before breakfast and each evening after supper I prayed:
"And lead us not into temptation but deliver us from evil."
The opportunity to do wrong was an ever present reality and the ability to resist, an unlikely truth. Worst of all was the punishment: Dad's.
One day I overheard Dad talking to Uncle Matthew. "This is a shit," Dad said, referring to an incident with the 'English' man over some chore with his bulldozer the stranger had not completed, as agreed. I was astounded. I stood trembling and stared at Dad with a distressed and inquiring expression on my face. Not long before Dad had given me a nasty beating for saying "shit."
"Christy, don't ever let me hear you use that word again," Dad said as he whipped me. "That's a bad word and I'll punish you every time you say it! Do you understand, Christy?"
"Yes, Dad," I said.
I ran and told Rebecca what I heard. She in turn told Mom. That evening before supper Mom confronted Dad.
"Davie," she said, "Christy heard you say a bad word today." She was upset and anxious. Dad, his annoyance evident

in his taut facial muscles, denied the incident and dismissed it with a lie.

"That's not so," he said, "the boy's telling another fib! I have to straighten him out!" He called me over and beat me in front of the entire family for tattling, or as he put it "telling a fib." I was embarrassed and humiliated: Again.

I remember, however, it was not the bruises from the lashing that agonized but the shocking realization that Dad had lied. I no longer considered him my hero. Instead, in my thoughts, I started to question his integrity.

"Dad is a liar….Dad is a LIAR!" I screamed again and again. The words churned over and over in my mind. I was now seven, impressionable and vulnerable. I neither understood nor knew how to handle this new situation. I was confused and I was bothered. I wanted answers but didn't know the right questions to ask or to whom I should turn. However, despite the agonizing uncertainties, I was sure something had changed forever that day. Something was shattered, something was lost: Something that could be neither repaired nor redeemed. The seed was fertilized.

※ ※ ※

In the Old Order Amish Community education was limited to eight years of grammar school. Students learned to read and write English and German. They also learned basic math, history, elementary science and geography. Afterwards girls worked in the house under the guidance of their mothers and boys either helped their dads on the farm or took a position as an apprentice to learn a trade. I recall quite vividly my school years because they left me with many painful memories.

Old Order Amish school houses were one room buildings in which all level classes assembled together. The mixture of children was interesting and we all knew each other despite our age differences.

I remember in the first grade I had a problem with Enis who at the time was fourteen years old and an eighth grader. He was a strong, mean-spirited boy with dark hair and a loud voice who liked to bully the younger boys. Somehow I annoyed him because I was short, pigeon-toed and had white hair.

One day while playing ship-wrecked, a game similar to baseball but with only three bases (home, middle and last), I slipped and fell. Enis laughed and shoved me against the wall while we were leaving the classroom.

"Dumb Enis," I shouted at him minutes later in front of his friends during recess. "You're just a big dumb boy who picks on little kids!" After school Enis got together with his buddies, a group of boys of various ages. They pounced on me, twisted my arms and pinned them behind my back. I was defenseless.

"Let's tie him up so we can teach him a lesson," Enis said. "He's a funny looking boy who can't even run without tripping and falling all over his own feet."

They dragged me behind the school house, away from the teacher's view. The sharp pebbles strewn along the road scratched my back and legs. The boys, snickering, tied me up with a thick coarse rope. I struggled to break away but was completely overpowered. My wrists burned from the friction of the rope and I noticed a small trickle of blood roll down into the palm of my right hand. I bent to the side and it dripped to the ground, coloring a white pebble crimson. Unconcerned, Enis and another boy equipped with sticks and the energy of outrage gave me a mean thrashing.

I was in pain, humiliated and terrified of Enis, but remained silent. My back was sore and throbbed from the continuous slam of the sticks. When the boys satisfied their mischievous whim, they ran off, proud of the whipping they had given me.

The brusies healed but the beating remained in my mind to haunt me.

"I'll show them," I said to myself. "They can't hurt me and get away with it!" It was an unrelenting torment: I had to get revenge or I would not have peace.

"Big dumb Enis's going to pay for what he did to me!" I said to myself.

I walked down the road and gathered some sharp edged

rocks. I threw them into the ditch, enjoying the echoing thump as each one hit bottom. Then with the tip of my right foot, I kicked in another two. After class with my heart racing and my intention set on revenge, I ran down the road and jumped into the ditch. I was prepared for the ambush.

I spotted Enis walking down the road with a couple of his friends. They were talking and laughing and swinging their empty lunch pails. I held my breath. My heart pounded. Tiny beads of sweat formed on my forehead.

Enis and the boys came closer and closer until they were within ten feet from where I was hiding. I sprang up and hurled my rocks: Anger was my strength, revenge my energy.

The first stone fell short and missed its target while the second cut a hole in Enis's pants, grazing his calf. The third hit him directly in the head.

He was stunned by the unexpected thud.

"Hey, what's going on?"

"Stop it!" he shouted, dropping his lunch pail.

I saw Enis shrink back in pain. His hand went to his head, perhaps to see if the rock had drawn blood. Although at the time I did not know, the rock had left a deep gash in his forehead.

I ran from the ditch, across the field to the barn. My heart raced as I went up to the hay mow. "I'll be safe here," I thought.

Peeking from the safety of my hiding place, I spotted Enis and the boys coming up the road. I stood frozen, holding my breath, fearful they had come to tell Mom of my wicked ambush. Instead, they passed right along without stopping.

I came back down from the hay mow and went to the house, relieved. That evening I sat down to supper pretending nothing had occurred. Revenge had muffled my pain. It may not have been the right thing to do, but it certainly made me feel good.

Later that evening, after supper, Teacher Aaron came for a visit. He was a tall, slender, young married man with red hair and a matching pointed eight inch beard. When I heard his voice, I knew I was in serious trouble. Aaron was Enis's brother. He came over to inform Dad about my rock throwing. I was in for a big lashing!

"Christy," Dad shouted, "get over here, right now. Teacher Aaron tells me you did a real bad thing today. Do you know your naughty behavior could have cost Enis an eye?"

By the sharp tone of his voice I knew Dad was infuriated. That evening, he gave me my first severe beating. Instead of the usual three or four lashes on my lower back, I received six. It hurt. It burned. It smarted. I was humiliated. I was embarrassed. I was angry. However, I was not sorry. I knew I'd hit Enis again if he ever tried to bully me.

The feeling of getting even was neat. It soothed my aches, all of them, the physical and the emotional.

After my assault on Enis and the boys, life at school became a misery. They got even with me. They poked fun at me because I was pigeon-toed. They laughed and scorned me for not being able to run during the ship-wreck games. They teased me because I was short and because my hair was white.

One day, excited about finally making a home run, I tripped over my own feet, came crashing to the ground and scratched my nose and face badly. I was unable to play for weeks until my bruises healed. I felt ill at ease, awkward and embarrassed about being pigeon-toed. The mocking continued. I was miserable and lonely. I felt isolated and cut off. I knew I was unlike the others, but I didn't quite understand why or what made me so different.

The unknown troubled me. It frustrated me. It puzzled me. It pushed me to explore further. I had to understand and I had to have answers.

Memories are hard to erase: Both the good and the bad. I never forgot old Buster, our beige collie farm dog. He was elderly and well liked but did not enjoy being patted. Buster opened his mouth, curled up his lips and snapped at the children if they tried to touch him. Around the farm he had a reputation for stealing and eating eggs. He loved to go into the barn, grab a couple in his mouth, run off and enjoy them in his private hideaway. Dad would hit him with a stick if he caught him or if we would report his misdeed.

I remember one particular morning when Dad was busy

doing chores. Rebecca and I spotted Buster roaming in the chicken house.

"Buster's in the chicken house again," I said to Rebecca, "I bet he stole some chicken eggs. We have to give him a lashing, 'cause Dad will do it anyway. Let's take him to the barn. Help me Rebecca."

"OK," she answered, "It'll be easier there, and we won't disturb Dad."

We coaxed Buster out from the chicken house and lured him into the barn.

Once inside, I tried to stick his head into one of the stanchions used for keeping the cows' heads steady during milking. The stanchions were four feet high steel posts about ten inches wide. There was a sixteen inch space at the top, which opened to slide the animal's head in. Once in place, it would close with a latch.

By now Buster sensed something and was nervous.

"Rebecca, Buster's too fidgety today. He must know something's up. I can't hold him steady. Go over to the shelf and get me some twine. I'll try to tie him down."

When Rebecca handed me the twine I quickly grabbed Buster's head, encircling it within my arms. He kicked and protested, knocking his snout against my chin. Warm sticky saliva ran down the side of my face.

"Phew," I said. "Buster must have eaten a lot of eggs. His breath stinks."

"Well, he doesn't have a tooth brush, so you can't expect him to clean his teeth," Rebecca said giggling. We both laughed at the thought of Buster brushing his teeth.

With Rebecca's help I tied Buster and fastened him to the milk stanchion. He whined and growled from fear and from the anticipation of the awful but all too familiar ritual about to take place. Rebecca gave him the first swat. I snatched the stick from her hand and continued to flog him.

"You're too soft, Rebecca," I said. "I've seen Dad do it. He hits hard and he swats fast!"

Buster's fur stood up with every lashing. It broke loose from his hide and flew around, rising, floating and falling. My pants were covered with his matted fur. The golden strands were a striking contrast against the heavy black material.

I felt sorry for Buster, but he was naughty and, like the rest of us who get caught misbehaving, he had to be beaten: Beatings were a memorable occurrence for both children and animals. They were feared and they were expected. They were a vital part of growing up: The solution to a problem and a means of educating. That's what I was taught to believe and that's what I believed until I discovered otherwise.

❊   ❊   ❊

CHAPTER 3

Lessons were taught through the sermons Dad and the Preachers preached in Church on Sundays and lessons were learned, observing their behavior and imitating their daily actions. This method of instruction confused and puzzled me. It forced me to analyze, to question and later to rebel. My behavior, however, began to reflect free thinking and, at seven, I started to walk towards an independent path. The double standard which put teachings in conflict with actions disturbed me, pulling me further away from the community.

Following the violent ways of others, I continued to amuse myself, killing chickens. Yet, once the thrill of doing something naughty and forbidden had subsided, I would dig a hole, lay them to rest and look for another way to find excitement.

One day while Dad was milking, Fritz crossed directly in front of him. In his mouth a dead chicken dangled. The odor of decayed meat filled the barn. Swarms of flies and mosquitoes hovered around Fritz.

Angry and fed up with the animal's repeated misbehavior, Dad grabbed the dog and gave him a severe beating.

"Fritz, I'm sick and tired of you killing the chickens," he shouted, flogging him on the back with a stick. The wood crackled every time it hit the dog's backbone. I grimaced with every whack, imagining Fritz's agony. At first he let out a grumble then as the pain increased, he dropped his chicken to snarl and howl.

"How many times have I told you to stay out of the chicken house?" Dad said.

Unable to defend himself, Fritz took the beating and limped out of the barn. I noticed his head was tilted down and his tail no longer wagged. It was tightly tucked between his hind legs. Several rows of black and white fur lay flat across his back. There were three circular bald patches, red and irritated from the force of the stick. I felt sorry for poor Fritz, knowing he was innocent. He did not kill the chicken, and I knew he did not deserve the beating. Despite my guilty conscience, I was too scared to do the right thing. I did not confess my sin to Dad.

Several days later, Mom and Dad reached a decision about Fritz. His routine of stealing and eating eggs had become too troublesome. And now he had killed another chicken. That evening Uncle Ben came to the house.

"Christy, come help me find Fritz," Uncle Ben said.

"Why, Uncle Ben?" I asked puzzled. "What do you want Fritz for?"

"Just do as I say," he replied. "I want to take him out behind the barn. Get me some twine."

"OK, Uncle Ben," I said, excited he had let me come along.

We took Fritz out behind the hog house.

"What are we going to do with him, Uncle Ben?" I said.

"We're going to wind some twine around his neck," he replied.

"Give me the twine, Christy."

I did as I was told, got the twine and handed it to Uncle Ben. It felt coarse and had a musty scent. Together we tied up Fritz and fastened him to a tree. He resisted, yelping and struggling to get loose. The twine was wound too tightly and his continued battle just intensified his agony. The more he kicked and squirmed, the deeper the twine cut into his neck.

"Uncle Ben, are you going to whip Fritz?" I asked, glancing at the rifle he was carrying.

"Be quiet and do as I say," he replied. Unhappy, I looked at Fritz, bound to the tree. His eyes flashed me a sad look. He was fidgety and still fighting to break free. The whimpers turned to wails and made me anxious. I knew Fritz was scared.

"Christy," Uncle Ben said, "I'm going to shoot Fritz! I hear he keeps stealing eggs and now he's killed another chicken. Your Mom and Dad have had it with him." He looked at Fritz then fixed his gaze on the rifle.

"But...Uncle Ben."

"But nothing, Christy: Be quiet and do as you're told," he said.

Taking Dad's Twenty-Two Marlin Bolt Action rifle in his hands, Uncle Ben positioned himself ten or twelve paces from Fritz and lifted the gun, resting the stock on his shoulder. He took a deep breath and opened fire. I was standing close to Fritz, just about six paces away. The blast of gunfire was ear shattering. I remained paralyzed, too frightened even to breathe. When I took my next breath, I felt my throat burn from the fumes of the gunpowder.

Blood first oozed, then sprayed and poured from Fritz's injuries, creating a gruesome scene. He was howling and snarling in agony, his wounded body writhing in pain. His big dark eyes, glassy and tearing, pleaded for compassion. I knew Fritz was in excruciating misery. It bothered me. I felt sick to my stomach.

"Hurry, Christy, run back to the house," Uncle Ben yelled, "I need more bullets to finish him off!" For a moment, his words freed me from my thoughts. With my heart pounding, I raced over to the barn.

"Dad," I shouted, "Uncle Ben needs more bullets. Dad, where are the bullets? Uncle Ben has no more bullets!"

"Calm down, Christy," Dad said, handing me the bullets. "Here, hurry now and give them to Ben."

I wondered if he knew what Uncle Ben was doing to Fritz, or more importantly, how he was doing it!

I snatched the bullets from Dad's hand and raced back to Uncle Ben.

"Uncle Ben, Dad gave me the bullets!" I shouted.

"Christy, put the bullets in the gun," he said, passing me the rifle. His eyes darted back to Fritz. They were cold and sinister. Fritz whimpered. He was trembling from fright and from pain. Uncle Ben chuckled then snickered. I didn't understand why he thought this was funny. The rifle was heavy, the metal icy. Holding it scared me. But I did as Uncle Ben asked and loaded it, keeping one eye on Fritz. Seeing him bloody and in pain I swallowed hard, fighting the tears swelling in my eyes.

Uncle Ben reached over and grabbed the rifle from my hands. His shirt was drenched across his back. I noticed two patchy yellow stains, one under each arm. When he came close and moved his arms, he stunk.

"Give me the gun," he said. "Are you dreaming, Christy? If you're scared you can go back to the house." With the loaded rifle secure on his shoulder, he took several steps towards Fritz.

"I'll finish you off now, you nasty beast," he said. Sneering, he raised the rifle. I looked down at Fritz. He was a bloody mess. Earlier Uncle Ben had shot several large holes in his belly.

Uncle Ben fired again. "I'll get you now," he said. The crackle of gun fire interrupted my thoughts. This time Uncle Ben aimed directly at the dog's head and neck, emptying the rifle.

Fritz heaved, sighed and stiffened. He was gone. His tongue, soaked with blood, drifted to the left side of his mouth, covered his lower teeth and hung over his bottom lip. It was ghastly. But it was over! Uncle Ben couldn't hurt Fritz again. His punishment was ended.

I felt appalled and wanted to get away. The pungent smell of gun powder lingered and made me queasy. I turned my back on Fritz, and ran over to the machine shed. I wanted to think about what had happened. In my mind, I replayed the grim scene over and over. Questions: I had so many questions! I needed answers.

"Why didn't Uncle Ben shoot Fritz in the head the first time? Why did he shoot him the belly, tormenting him? Why did he look at him and chuckle as he lay there agonizing?" I asked myself. He did not have to let him die a slow torturous death.

The sight of Fritz, bleeding, howling and writhing in agony, disturbed me. Uncle Ben could have killed the dog quickly. What he did was sickening. Today, I disliked him even more than usual. Hatred was growing within me.

After supper I went back down and around the barn to check on Fritz. It was summer and the sun had not yet set. In the glow of early dusk I spotted him still fastened, lifeless. Carefully I untied the knot around his neck, loosened the twine and gently guided his head to the ground. He seemed to be resting more comfortably. I poked him with a stick lying nearby to be certain he was dead.

Fritz was ice cold and motionless. Droves of insects swarmed about buzzing and gnawing at his flesh.

Leaning over I noticed the wide holes in his belly, neck and head.

"Uncle Ben could have shot him once in the head," I said to myself. "He's cruel. He's a mean man. I don't like Uncle Ben!"

That evening I remained sleepless. I felt responsible for what happened to Fritz. I knew he was put down for something I had done. I tossed and turned in my bed, feeling the sting of guilt. I wondered if I should confess my wrong doing to Dad.

"Maybe I'll feel better if I tell him the truth," I thought aloud. However, I knew the whipping I would receive as a result of my confession would be brutal, painful and vicious. The thought sent a shudder through my body. I decided to keep my misdeed a secret. It was easier and it didn't hurt; at least not physically. Eventually I would get a whipping anyway, for one reason or another! It seemed to be my fate. I turned over, buried my head in the pillow and waited for a new day.

Week day mornings always included attending school. Some days were good and others were bad. One of my classmates was a retarded boy named Alvin, a nervous, high strung child with a wild look in his eyes. Besides his own difficulties, Alvin had serious problems with his dad. Because of his troublesome family situation, he would frequently arrive late for classes. Teacher

Aaron would not start the lessons until everyone was present and we became restless waiting.

I remember one morning we were all seated and ready for class but Alvin had not yet arrived. Teacher Aaron went to the door to see if he was on his way. He yanked it open to get a better view. At that moment Alvin came running in, his face beet red.

"Dad's drunk, Dad's drunk!" he yelled. We laughed and mimicked him, imitating his words. "Dad's drunk, Dad's drunk," we chanted in chorus.

"Be quiet. Quit laughing!" Teacher Aaron said, slamming his fist on the desk. "Stop it!" he shouted as the giggling continued. He walked over to Alvin, put his hand on the boy's shoulder and reassured him and the rest of us that this was not true.

"Alvin, your dad is not drunk. He must be sick!"

"No," Alvin replied, "Dad's not sick, Dad's got the shits, and he's drunk!"

Amused, the class burst into laughter. Teacher Aaron again called for silence.

"Be quiet, and stop this nonsense," he said. "You're here to learn." His face was red from excitement.

"You'll all get a lashing if you continue carrying on like this," he said. "Do you understand?" No one responded.

"Everyone is present and it's time for lessons. Let's get busy," he said.

Teacher Aaron motioned for the first graders to come forward.

"Sit here," he said pointing his index finger to an old wooden bench near his desk.

Shuffling his feet, Alvin took a seat on the bench alongside the rest of us. He was flustered and excited. His wide-opened eyes darted around the room. Teacher Aaron turned to him and said,

"Alvin, please recite the vowels." The boy twitched, still agitated and jumped to his feet.

"I can't," he said. "I gotta shit."

"Stop this nonsense Alvin," Teacher Aaron said. "Do you want a spanking in front of the whole school? I'm warning you!"

"No, no, Teacher Aaron," Alvin shouted. "I really gotta shit. I mean it. I gotta shit and my belly hurts."

Teacher Aaron, his angry gaze fixed on Alvin, grabbed the strap from his desk. The boy began to sob.

"OK, Alvin," he said, "We'll walk through the vowels together. I'll help you." Teacher Aaron began, "A...E.. I..." Alvin stuttered and stumbled a few times then, frustrated, said, "I can't do this 'cause I really gotta shit!"

"Enough, Alvin, now you're going to get it. I've had all I can take," Teacher Aaron said. "Stand up!" The boy scrambled to his feet, his red hair stood at attention. Picking up the three foot leather strap, Teacher Aaron unrolled it and flogged Alvin's bottom. He then released him from the class to take care of his need.

Several minutes later, Teacher Aaron's words were interrupted by a crackling squeak. I turned in time to see the old wooden school door swing open. Alvin stuck his head in.

"I gotta shit some more. My belly still hurts," he yelled. "I gotta go back out."

"Alvin, get over here," Teacher Aaron said irritated. "You're creating a disturbance and I'm going to give you a whipping." Alvin turned and fled. He ran down the road and away from the school. The class burst into laughter. Teacher Aaron tried to end the ruckus.

"I want you all to know, it is forbidden to leave the school grounds," he said.

"Alvin will get a severe lashing from his dad for running off. Anyone else who disobeys and leaves will also get punished."

Threats of physical violence were a common part of growing up; an eerie rite of passage, always carried out as threatened. They were amends for wrong doings and considered a fair and justifiable retribution. The time and place did not matter. The house, the barn, school even my beloved out-doors were all suitable settings for lashings: Church was no exception.

It was a bright Sunday morning. Customarily two Sundays a month we attended Church service. Dad was a Bishop, the highest position in the Old Order Amish Community. He set the rules and led his flock by intimidation and authority. His power was neither questioned nor contradicted: Not at this point in time; and certainly not by me.

The Old Order Amish did not worship in official Churches. Therefore, Sunday services were held in the houses of different people in the community. The men would gather together in one room and the women in another, usually the kitchen. The Bishops and Preachers delivered the sermons, instructing their flock to live according to the writings in the Bible and the traditions of the Old Order Amish Community.

I remember having to sit for three hours on a rigid bench while the Preachers and Dad delivered their sermons. Sitting still for a lengthy period was uncomfortable and it aggravated my weak back. Suffering repeated lashings while still a small child resulted in chronic back injuries and chronic pain. After a half hour, I would swing my feet and arch my spine. The motion would relieve some of the stress and offer an outlet for my pent up energy.

One Sunday, Dad caught me swinging my legs and swaying from side to side. He grabbed me by the ear and took me outside to the shed.

"Christy, I've told you over and over to sit still in Church," he said. "Don't you listen when I speak to you? The Lord is upset with those who don't obey!" His furrowed brow betrayed the force of his rage. I gazed down at my feet, accomplices to my misdeed. I was scared and as always I began to cry. I knew it was useless but it was better than answering Dad. Whatever I said mattered little and often resulted in getting more lashes.

Irritated, Dad grabbed me by the ear and yanked me over.

"Stop it, Christy," he said, "This crying and fussing isn't going to work! You hear me!"

"Yes, Dad," I said. He swatted me across the face. His calloused palm slammed into my right cheek and with a quick swing, backhanded my left one. The sound of the slaps echoed, competing with my sobs.

"Get back to Church, Christy," Dad said. I returned to Church with my face a scarlet ball. It swelled and it stung. I came in and took my seat. Distracted by the sounds of my scuffling footsteps, every head turned. I was embarrassed, humiliated and in pain. This was Dad's intention.

Sunday was always a different day, a very special day and a time for prayer and for calling on family and friends. Sometimes on Sundays we would go over to Grandpa Kemp's to visit and attend service at his Church. My maternal Grandpa was a heavy-set man with warm dark eyes. A twelve inch salt and pepper beard outlined his round face creating a dramatic look against the dark complexion.

Grandpa Kemp lived in an area of the community where the Young Folks delighted in racing their horses up and down the road. From Grandpa's porch I had a great view of the road and could easily see the action.

The clinking of hooves and billows of dust rising as the animals raced by excited me. On dry days, the speckles of sand kicked up, sometimes tickled my nose and made me sneeze. But I loved to watch this fast paced event. As always, I was keyed up and eager to see who would win. The Young Folks cheered their horses and their animated voices were exhilarating. It was a thrilling happening!

My Grandpa Burkholder and my Uncle Ben gained neither my respect nor my affections. However, my memories of Uncle Mahlon Kemp were always heartwarming. I always looked up to him as a role model. Uncle Mahlon was my hero; he was fun and he was cool. I enjoyed his animated sense of humor and found his often bold behavior inspiring and worth imitating.

Uncle Mahlon was a hefty, robust man with a wild, side-splitting laugh. When he chuckled his chest would puff out and rattle. His whimsical eyes would crinkle at the corners, taking on a particular glow, especially when he was in a mischievous mood.

Uncle Mahlon was married to a petite, slender woman. The couple's physical differences were comical and created quite a hilarious contrast when they were together. Every time they rode in their courting buggy, I noticed it would dip dangerously on the side where Uncle Mahlon sat. This amused me and I would tease him relentlessly.

One Sunday, standing in front of Church before service I saw Uncle Mahlon come down the road in his buggy at an accelerated pace. Reckless speed was frowned upon in the community. It was dangerous and the noise disturbed the serene atmosphere.

Suddenly, with a swift pull of the rein, Uncle Mahlon yanked his horse, forcing him to change direction. The buggy turned sharply, riding on two wheels for a brief second. The clang of splattering rocks broke the early morning stillness. I watched, fascinated, as a huge cloud of dust and soot covered the buggy. A crowd of onlookers gathered, curious to see what all the uproar was about. Uncle Mahlon, proud of his actions, greeted the crowd with a broad grin.

I loved Uncle Mahlon's outgoing personality.

"Cool! I want to be just like Uncle Mahlon when I grow up," I said. "I won't care what anybody says or thinks."

Early on I admired people who were different, people who stood up for their ideas and feelings, people like Uncle Mahlon who were not fearful of being themselves. These individuals were an inspiration, because in the Amish community, differences in thought and behavior were rare, unacceptable and often signaled trouble. Anything that was unusual and swerved from common routine did not pass unobserved and was frowned upon. It was a collective society in which differences from the norm were scorned.

Buggies were the main source of transportation in the Old Order Amish Community. They were predominately unadorned black coaches, pulled by a buggy horse. Courting buggies were small and accommodated two people whereas standard buggies were large enough to hold a family. Buggy horses were vital and tended to with diligence because they served a purpose for daily survival. Unfortunately they often faced cruel abuse either for misbehaving or simply because someone sought to even the score. Mistreating and harming a man's animal was how anger and misdeeds were vindicated.

Red was a short-built, light red buggy horse. He was nervous and often a bit stubborn in refusing to pull. One Sunday, after service he was particularly obstinate and unwilling to obey a command. We were all seated in the buggy and ready for the return ride to the house. Red refused to take off, despite Dad's insistent coaxing. He pulled back and nervously shuffled his hooves. After several minutes of baulking he attempted to rise on his hind legs. The fussing broke the morning calm and an audience of onlookers gathered.

I looked at Red and noticed he had a raw open sore on his shoulder, resulting from a poorly fitted collar. The pads had caused a serious irritation which made him anxious. I wondered why no one thought to get him a better harness.

Dad jumped from the buggy and unhitched Red.

"I'll teach you a lesson," he said bending over the horse's ear. Dad held him firm with one hand.

"Get the buggy whip!" he shouted to the Elders who were leaving Church. "I've got a bad horse."

Red was immediately given ten or twelve lashes. He winced in agony, becoming more agitated. After the beating, believing he had resolved the problem, Dad hooked Red back to the buggy with the help of the Elders. Once again Red baulked and refused to pull. Without warning, he reared up and threw himself on the ground with a loud thud.

"He's possessed! We need to break his spirit," one of the Elders said to Dad.

In a few minutes Red was unhitched; his harness brutally yanked off. I was terrified. I feared for Red. I was confused by the Elder's words and didn't quite understand how they would "break his spirit." However, I was sure Red was in for a nasty time. He disobeyed Dad. He went against his wishes and I knew what that meant. I clenched my teeth and felt my stomach churn. The feeling was not good. Violence was always appalling. But brutality was Dad's way of dealing with disobedience.

Four or five Elders ran over to Red. Their eagerness to whip him was evident in their sneers. I heard a harsh voice;

"Let's knock him to the ground. Then we'll fix him up."

Two of the Elders jumped on Red's back and the remaining encircled him. They pushed and shoved until he crashed to the ground. He went down, defenseless under the strength of their aggression.

Once prostrate, two Elders pounced on Red's head, while another grabbed his tail and, with a forceful tug, pulled it towards his head.

Red was pinned to the ground. He was helpless. He had to await his terrible fate in agony.

The Elders filled a five gallon bucket with water.

"Pour the water down his nose," one of the Elders said. "Hurry we can't hold him down forever. That'll teach him to stop baulking!"

They lifted Red's head and emptied the bucket down his nose. The horse struggled and gasped. His large dark eyes bulged and darted from side to side. I could see the fear and the pain.

"Get the buggy whip," another Elder shouted. "We're not finished with him yet!" Red was given a few more lashings. I clenched my fists as I listened, horrified, to the loud whisking sounds of the whip hitting against Red's back. I saw his skin split open where the leather had sliced into the hair. Blood was spilling out from his head wounds. I was sickened. I began sobbing.

"Mom….Mom," I said, "Is Red going to be OK? He's bleeding and whimpering. Mom, I'm scared. Why are Dad and the Elders whipping him?"

"Christy, he'll be just fine," she said. "Red is misbehaving and upsetting your Dad."

The Elders continued to beat Red until he was exasperated. He emitted a piercing shriek and settled back motionless.

Satisfied with Red's outburst the Elders stepped aside.

"We have broken his bad spirit!" They said, nodding their heads in agreement.

Red started to fidget. Quivering he gasped for air. His tongue was thrust forward and coated with blood. He was probably thirsty after his atrocious ordeal. One of the Elders walked over, looked down, snickered and gave him a swift kick in the back. I winced feeling his pain.

Red immediately stood up. His legs, trembling and weak from the cruel beating, could not hold his weight. He crashed down to the ground.

"Get up, Red," Dad commanded. He was holding the lead rope and gave the horse another lashing. Red stood, unsteady on his legs. Without any compassion for his wounds, he was forced into his harness and hitched to the buggy.

Dad took the reins and we continued down the road. Red did not baulk. He continued his course at a slow unsteady trot. I questioned Dad's violent ways.

Later that evening while finishing my milking chores, I went over to Red's stall to check on him. He had refused to eat and stood listless with his head down. His eyes were sad. I went over, patted his face and glanced at his wounds. He had large open welts, encrusted with dried blood from the lashing, and deep raw sores from his badly fitted collar. I walked over to the side of the stall and picked up the bag balm. This was an ointment Dad used when the cows had chapped udders. It was cooling and soothing.

I rubbed the balm into Red's cuts. He winced and recoiled and I lightened my touch, realizing he was in agonizing pain. After a few moments he settled down and seemed to find comfort in my gentle touch. The menthol fragrance of the balm calmed him. He sighed and nuzzled his clammy nose up and down my arm. It was his way of saying thank you. I was relieved but still devastated and angry. I knew I would never forget the brutality I witnessed that morning.

Dad's rules were enforced through aggression. Disobedience upset him and was treated with corporal punishment. It was his rule for children and animals. He believed it was justified. That was the Bishop's way. I did not understand the violence, disagreed and began to pull away from Dad.

✻   ✻   ✻

CHAPTER 4

I continued learning about life by listening to and observing the behavior of those around me. Life was still new and the many unknowns I was beginning to uncover encouraged me to explore and experiment. I was upset with Dad, having discovered he did not always tell the truth even though he continued to whip me for lying. His truth was a "broken truth."

The violent behavior intensified and I imitated the aggressive ways of others, determined to resolve my own problems and heal my own injuries through vindictive actions. I realized something was not right. The confusion I felt pushed me to investigate further and continue to seek new adventures and more importantly to find answers.

Isaac Burkholder was my cousin and best friend. He was a slender, good looking boy with dark hair and eyes. We enjoyed many fishing and hunting outings together and were inseparable. Although Isaac had a sprightly sense of humor, he was a silent reflective type. I would talk and he would always listen to what I had to say.

One afternoon, while putting up hay, the men gathered under a large oak tree to enjoy a shady refuge during their mid day beak. Putting up hay was not a very pleasant chore, especially during the hot, humid summer months.

To put up hay, we used a wagon that was eight feet wide and fourteen feet long, pulled by two sturdy Belgian horses. A hay loader was attached to the rear of the wagon. The hay was put in windrows and formed into long rolls. The hay loader then picked up the windrows and slid them ten feet in the air, dropping the hay in the bed of the wagon.

While the men continued their mid-day break, Isaac and I headed for a new adventure. We left, picked up a couple of sticks, and raced over to the hog lot to chase the hogs.

"Isaac," I said, pointing my finger, "Go after that fat one. Hurry, don't let him get away. Hit him on the butt. Let's see how fast he can go."

I ran alongside Isaac as he swatted the hog and chased him through the lot. We were sweaty from putting up hay, and our dark pants were covered with strands of hay.

"I gotta pee!" Isaac said laughing. He unbuttoned his fly and relieved himself.

"Do you want to touch it, Christy?" Isaac said showing me his penis.

"I don't know," I said, not knowing what to say.

"C'mon, Christy, touch my penis. It feels really good. You'll see 'cause then I'll touch yours." Puzzled but intrigued by his invitation I stepped closer. I extended my hand and patted his penis.

"Not like that, Christy," Isaac said.

"Then how, Isaac?" I said.

"Unbutton your pants, Christy, and I'll show you," Isaac said.

"I've never done this before, Isaac." I was anxious but curious. I obeyed his wishes and unbuttoned my pants. Nervous, I pulled too hard and one the buttons popped off. Isaac laughed then took my penis in his hands and stroked it firmly and vigorously.

"Isaac, that feels good!" I said. "Where did you learn how to do that?"

"My brother James showed me," he said.

"Christy, now it's my turn. Put your hands around my penis and slide them up and down like I did."

He stood directly in front of me. I obeyed and gave Isaac the same pleasure he had given me. Later that evening I became restless, thinking about what Isaac and I had done. The tingling sensation I felt was thrilling. However, shortly thereafter, I was bothered by the thought that perhaps my game with Isaac was wrong.

"Maybe Isaac and I did a bad thing," I said to myself as I walked back to the house. That evening I was restless and had an awful nightmare about poor Fritz!

※ ※ ※

One day, soon after, we were putting up hay for Grandpa. Rebecca was driving the hay rack and I stood beside her. While I backed the team up to the hay loader, Uncle Ben approached.

"Rebecca, come over here," He said. "I need your help." She obeyed, jumped down and came around behind him.

"A little closer," Uncle Ben said, motioning to her with his hand.

She was now directly in front of him. Uncle Ben hooked up the hay loader then turned abruptly. He reached from behind and grabbed Rebecca's crotch with his sweaty hand. He pulled her to him. Uncle Ben's face, flushed with excitement, betrayed his lust. He shoved his hand between her legs, making his way to her underpants. His breathing was rapid and heavy as he fondled her genitals, digging, groping and massaging the young girl. With his free hand he probed and rubbed her butt. Both hands were moving; caressing, feeling and thrusting. The panting continued. The ten year old girl's body aroused him. He grinned, revealing a heavily discolored set of teeth. His eyes bulged. He looked rather unsightly and a bit scary. After several minutes, Uncle Ben forced Rebecca hard against his body and held her tightly. Satisfied with the pleasure he stole from her, he lifted her, setting her back on the wagon.

"Bet you enjoyed that, Rebecca," he said chuckling. "Did I tickle you enough?"

Uncle Ben habitually touched and fondled young girls. I was disgusted by his perverted actions. The sight of him sickened me and I couldn't stand to be in his company.

"I'll show him," I said to myself. "I'll get even with him one day."

Uncle Ben lived with Grandpa Burkholder. Both men disturbed me and made me anxious. I didn't know which of the two I disliked more.

One Sunday, feeling irritated with Grandpa, I said to Isaac, "Let's take Grandpa's dog out back." Isaac agreed and we lured Rover into following us. Once outside we enclosed him in a circular wired bin. We climbed in, chased him around and beat him with sticks. Rover was howling and yelping as we continued swatting his back. Hearing the ruckus, Dad came running.

"Christy, what are you doing to Grandpa's dog?" he said.

Not waiting for a response he yanked me by the ear and threw me a swift hard slap across the face. I felt my ear go numb and my cheek burn. Despite the pain I did not regret my deed. Since I was not able to hit Grandpa, beating his dog was my way of getting revenge. Among the Amish it was customary to get even with someone who had committed a wrong by beating and injuring their animals. I did as I saw others do and not as I was told. Right or wrong, it always made me feel better.

There were many new occurrences and changes in the Amish community that were not in keeping with Dad's ideas and teachings. They worried and scared him. I remember one Saturday evening I overheard Mom and Dad talking in the front living room. I was lying in bed, and sat up abruptly to listen.

"Amelia," Dad said "I have some very disturbing news." Mom was silent, sighed and waited for Dad to continue.

"Amelia, there are bad people in this community: People who are drinking."

Mom gasped, becoming increasingly anxious with every word he said.

"Are you certain, Davie?" she said. "Maybe it's just a nasty rumor. You know how rumors get started and how quickly they spread."

"No, Amelia, there are also people driving cars with the 'English' folk!"

I heard Mom say, "Davie, this is a very serious matter. Do you know who they are? Who is drinking and driving cars? I'm afraid, Davie, this is dreadful news."

"Yes, Amelia," Dad said. "I'm fearful the situation is out of control. Evil has taken over this community. We must take the children and move away before it's too late. There is a bad spirit here; people are disobeying the Lord. They're pulling away!"

I sat motionless. I held my breath and clasped my hands tightly together. I was terrified. Dad always preached that when the Lord's Will is contradicted or denied the world will end. According to Dad when people reject and pull away from the Lord, they do bad things. Evil takes over their lives.

"We're going to the end," I thought! "The world is going to end!"

I was unable to sleep. I spent the night thinking about the drinking and the cars, contemplating how the world would end. Death was an unknown. I wondered what it would be like to die. The thought of being dead frightened me. Would it hurt? What will happen to me once I'm dead? What would I do when I died? My questioning mind had no boundaries. I needed answers, I wanted answers. I vowed one day I would have them.

Anger and hatred gave life to payback. Payback was accomplished through vindictive behavior. Violence swirled around me on a daily basis, through the lashings I received and the beatings I gave to animals in retaliation. Settling the score was a way of life: The Old Order Amish way.

My Uncle Ralph Burkholder was a middle-aged man with a curious, inquiring look permanently stamped on his face. He was slim, not very tall and wore a six inch black beard. He was Isaac and James' father.

While visiting Uncle Ralph for an overnight stay, Elma and I, together with cousins Isaac and James, entertained ourselves with a game called "cow playing." My sister, Elma Burkholder, born March 9, 1971, was Mom and Dad's second child. She was an attractive, dark-complexioned, short, plump girl who liked to listen when I spoke. Elma joined Rebecca and I and enjoyed the games we played.

"Cow playing" took place in the milking parlor of Uncle Ralph's barn. Excited, we would get down on all fours and crawl into the barn, like cows. The person who was to be "milked" was led into the barn by the person who would do the "milking." Once inside, their heads were placed in the stanchion and the latch was closed. They would then be "milked." Their genitals would be treated like udders, pulled and pinched through their clothes as if to draw milk. After the "milking," the roles would be reversed until everyone had a chance to "milk" and be "milked." This "cow playing" game was a fun way of engaging in childlike sexual experimentation. We touched and fondled each other in a naive manner, laughing and enjoying the game.

We received no formal sex education. It was not uncommon for a fifteen year old to believe babies were bought and brought back to the house to be raised. Among the Old Order Amish the word "sex" was never mentioned in front of children, and barely whispered in the company of adults. It was taboo; an unmentionable. Sins of the flesh were neither explained nor discussed. Instead they were defined and dismissed as a serious evil. Young people who indulged in any type of sexual conduct outside of marriage were severely whipped in retribution for the bad thing they had done. To me it seemed as if there were too many bad things. Everything fun was evil.

One Saturday evening, dark, murky smoke billowed from Grandpa Burkholder's straw stack, in the direction of the school yard. Rumor had it that some members of the Amish community had set the blaze seeking revenge. They wanted to get even with Grandpa for some wrong doing he had committed.

Dad rushed over along with Grandpa to smother the flames and survey the damage. Once the flames were suffocated, they looked for clues to confirm Grandpa's suspicion that it was arson.

"Davie," Grandpa said, "I want you to pursue this matter in Church on Sunday. I want answers and I want to know what's going on. I want to know who's responsible for setting the blaze and why they did it."

"OK," Dad said. "I'd like to know what's going on also. Blazes don't get set by themselves. We'll find out who's responsible."

The following day, in accordance with Grandpa's wishes, Dad called a special meeting. Dad, the Bishop, announced the straw stack fire in Church on Sunday. He called on Grandpa to state his case then interrogated him.

"Can you tell us what happened last evening?" he said.

"Someone set fire to my straw stack. It went up in a nasty blaze," Grandpa said, his anger visible in his accusing glance. His eyes darted around the room, searching for the arson.

"Were you able to gather any evidence?" Dad said. "Do you have any idea what actually happened or who could have been responsible?"

"Yeah, somebody right here in this Church room did it," Grandpa said. "I'll find out who did it." He rotated his eyes around the room.

"I want the guilty person to stand up right now," he continued. "Confess your sin and let's be done with it," he said in a final attempt to unmask the arson.

The room remained quiet. No one came forward to take the blame. Uncle Edwin stood alongside Grandpa and demanded a confession. In his role as an Elder in the Church, he repeated Grandpa's plea for the arsonist to stand and admit his wrong doing.

Silence prevailed. It was obvious no one was coming forward. Grandpa Burkholder, a powerful authoritarian Church member, was unsuccessful in drawing a confession from the young folks. His depleted power, his human failing pleased and delighted me: I had little if any respect for him and his violent, mean ways. Someone got even with Grandpa and got away with it. I was thrilled!

CHAPTER 5

It was a tranquil Sunday morning and Church was filled with people attending service. I was seated on a bench intent on looking around the room to see who was present. Distractions came often and were silent companions.

The screech of a horse and buggy nearing Church drowned the Preacher's sing song voice. I knew from the hurried clip-clops of the horse, it was traveling at a fast pace. The buggy came to a halt. Curious, I came to attention and waited to see who would come running through the door.

"Someone is late for service," I said to myself, wondering why. Tardiness for Sunday service was uncommon and not tolerated in the Old Order Amish Community: Something was very wrong and I was eager to learn what it was!

The door flung open and one of the young folk, Elmer Eicher came running in shouting for his dad. He was anxious and distressed and I noticed his hands twitched nervously. Under the wide brim of his hat, a frantic, blood-shot gaze showed fear and anguish. A steady stream of tears oozed from the corners of his eyes and trickled into the sparse hairs of his recently sprouted beard.

"Dad! Dad," he said, "Come quickly. Something bad has happened. Hurry, Dad!"

The boy's father, Simon Eicher, was a Preacher. The song had already been sung and he was seated on the bench alongside the Preachers. Simon turned to face his son. He sensed a serious problem had occurred, jumped to his feet and ran towards Elmer. The worried look appearing on his face made him seem older than his actual age. I was at full attention. My pulse quickened and my heart throbbed; I felt the excitement of anticipation.

The Bishop stopped preaching. Silence invaded the Church. Hurriedly father and son ran toward the door and jumped on the buggy. The Bishop raised his head and took up his sermon from where he had been unexpectedly interrupted. There was an unsettling feeling in the room. It was difficult to concentrate. My mind wandered. I had to know what was going on!

About an hour later, the door creaked then slid open. In walked Elmer's father. He removed his hat. His face was taut and flushed; his eyes glassy. With a determined gait he walked into the kitchen where his wife sat in the company of other women. Visibly troubled he bent over and whispered several words in her ear. She paled and followed her husband to the buggy.

Once again a strange hush permeated the room. It was an unusual stillness; not the soothing quiet of serenity. Every head turned in the direction of the Eichers as they departed Church.

Rumors are quick to be born and quick to spread. After the service, whispers carried the news that something terrible had happened to one of the Eichers. Elmer's younger brother Ruben had been killed! I was not satisfied with the one sentence explanation and as always pursued my quest for answers.

"Mom, what happened yesterday during Sunday service?" I said. "Why did Elmer come late to Church?" Not waiting for an answer I continued, "Why did Elmer's Dad race out of Church then come back to collect his family? Mom they left Church in such a rush. Did you see that?"

"Yes, Christy," Mom replied. "A terrible thing happened."

Mom settled herself down beside me, Rebecca and Elma and explained what had happened.

"After their dad left, Ruben and Elmer prepared themselves

for Church," she said. "They had argued earlier in the morning and were annoyed and irritated."

"What were they fighting about, Mom?" I said impatient to have all the answers.

"I don't know, Christy, but it doesn't matter. I know they were just angry with each other and fighting like brothers often do. Then Elmer spotted the rifle used for shooting birds. It was leaning up against a wall in a corner of the milk house. He grabbed it and jokingly pointed it at his brother."

"He shot Ruben! Is that what he did, Mom?" I said, my pulse racing.

"Not exactly, Christy," she said. "He was frantic and upset with Elmer and not thinking very clearly. Anger does that to you, Christy. That's why it's bad to get angry and fight."

"Then what happened, Mom?" I said

"In a moment of anger Elmer lost control and accidentally pulled the trigger. The gun fired and Ruben was killed instantly."

"What do you mean he accidentally pulled the trigger?" I said. "Elmer shot and killed his brother! If he pulled the trigger he shot him!" I continued, excited.

"Christy," Mom said, "Accidentally means he did not want to do it. It was an accident: A very sad accident."

"What will happen now, Mom?" I asked.

"There will be a funeral service for him and he will be buried," she said.

That evening I lay in bed, agitated and unable to sleep. My thoughts turned to Uncle Ben and the brutal way in which he shot Fritz.

"That was no accident," I said to myself. "Uncle Ben wanted to pull the trigger. He wanted to kill Fritz! I wonder if Elmer wanted to kill Ruben!"

In the Old Order Amish Tradition, funerals were conducted three days after the deceased had passed on. The service was somber and simple. There were no flowers and no eulogies. The casket was a six sided wooden box with a split lid.

Ruben Eicher's funeral was my first experience with death

and burials. I was both curious and excited. I was quiet during the service, listening and watching. At the conclusion of the service, everyone walked past Ruben's casket to pay their final respects. He was laid out for prayer and for viewing. I glanced in as we neared the casket and noticed a big black hole right in the center of Ruben's head. The uneven edges were blue and dark purple; a dramatic contrast against his ashen complexion. A chill went down my back. It looked so eerie. There was a weird aroma. It wasn't honeysuckles and it wasn't manure, but something in between. Maybe that's how dead people smelled, I thought and shrugged my shoulders.

I recalled Mom's story about Elmer killing his brother Ruben by accidentally shooting him in the head. This was like Cain and Abel:

"Cain turned against his brother Abel and slew him."

"I wonder if that was an accident, too," I thought to myself. "Maybe Cain did not want to kill Abel."

I heard Mom's words over and over: "Christy, anger is a bad thing." I took another look at Ruben with the huge black hole in his head. I took a deep breath, inhaled the mysterious aroma and shuddered. Afterwards Dad accompanied us to the buggy. Most of the families attending the service were also heading over to their buggies. The usual quiet aura was overcome with the sounds of crunching gravel and the clip-clops of departing horses.

Once on our buggies, we waited for the hack buggy to pull around. It was a buggy built with a trunk like bed in the rear. The casket was placed on this bed. When loaded, the buggy began its unhurried procession to the grave site.

The Bishop, the Preachers, the Deacons and Ruben's family proceeded behind the hack buggy. Seventy or eighty buggies followed. The procession moved down the road at a somber pace. The grinding echo of the rotating buggy wheels traveling along the road together with the steady thud of the horses' hooves shattered the silence.

Riding along the road, I noticed the passing 'English' decreased their speed, steered their cars over to the side and sat motionless as a sign of respect, The Elders always appreciated this valued gesture. It verified the 'English' man's reverence for Amish tradition.

The buggies were driven to the grave site, a sacred Amish burial ground. When they arrived, the horses were fastened to the fence and the buggies emptied.

"Christy, take off your hat and bow your head," Dad said. This time I did as I was told. I quickly glanced to my left, then to my right and noticed all the men were bareheaded and every head was bowed.

After the prayers two ropes were attached to the coffin, one at the head and one at the foot. Four men were called, all unrelated to the deceased.

"Dad, what's going to happen now?" I said.

"Be quiet, Christy," he said. "You'll see."

The four men lifted the casket while two others removed the wood plank on which it rested.

Gradually they lowered the casket into the hole. This was a signal for the people to begin departing.

"Dad what's happening?" I said.

"The men will throw dirt over the coffin, Christy," Dad said, "Until the hole is filled and the casket is completely buried."

Following the burial rite it was customary for the family to unite at the supper table to share a meal. Afterwards the Elders gathered to discuss the joy and feeling of serenity they experienced knowing the young man died as an Amish, in peace with God and Church. They looked upon his life as a noteworthy means of achieving salvation and felt elated in the certainty he now rested in the joy of harmony, redeemed and embraced by the Lord.

Grandpa Burkholder, stepping up to his position of authority as a Preacher, later addressed a group of people in the community. He used Ruben's passing as an example to explain how eternal salvation is attained through commitment to the Amish faith.

"Ruben's seat in heaven," he said, "is a reward for living a good life in observance of and obedient to the Amish Tradition."

He then cited some of the ex-Amish who had died, shunned and condemned. They passed on not in good favor with the Lord unlike Ruben who achieved salvation in death.

"Ruben Eicher," he said "lived a good and simple life, as an Amish young folk. He was neither rebellious nor critical of Church rule. He lived according to the Will of God expressed in the scriptures."

He paused, cleared his throat several times and continued.

"Ruben stood before his Creator, forgiven for all his wrong doings. He was judged for his merits, and granted salvation, unlike the ex-Amish who died in sin. They were shunned and condemned for abandoning their faith and betraying their families and community. They closed their eyes as evil men living among the wicked," Grandpa said, his voice harsh and reproachful.

"These ex-Amish have been thrown into darkness and forced to suffer eternal damnation," he said. "Their lives ended in the ban."

Softening his tone he concluded:

"But God called one of the Amish to join Him in heaven. Today is a special day and we feel happy knowing Ruben Eicher rests in peace, beside the Lord!"

My Uncle Edwin Burkholder was a short stocky man with a twelve inch salt and pepper beard. He had a false eye which he would remove to terrorize and intimidate, thinking he was cool. Although by nature he was a devious and hypocritical man, he was an Elder with an inclination toward spiritual fanaticism.

One day Uncle Edwin came racing to Grandpa Burkholder's on his horse.

"Hurry, come quick," he yelled to Grandpa. "My buggy shop is on fire!"

"Edwin, let's get over there before it spreads," Grandpa said running toward the barn to get his horse.

The men raced over to Uncle Edwin's. Huge billows of dark, murky smoke greeted them as they neared the shop. In the center, intense red-yellow flames cut through the clouds. The air was smoky and it was difficult to breathe. The crackling sound of smoldering wood overpowered the screams and howls of frightened men and animals.

The men, with the help of several neighbors, were able to restrain the blaze. They tossed buckets of water, drenching the flames until they were just flickering cinders, iridescent in the twilight. It was blistering and the men were soaked in sweat. Their hats and faces were covered with ashes and they smelled like slabs of charred meat.

"Edwin," Grandpa Burkholder said, "this fire in your buggy shop seems a bit suspicious to me."

"Do you think it was lit by the same person who set your straw stack on fire?" Uncle Edwin said to Grandpa.

"I don't have any evidence, but there is an evil person here in Bowling Green. Someone is doing bad things in this community," Grandpa said. "I'm going to call on the Bishop and have him assemble a special meeting at Church. We need to get to the bottom of this right away."

If Grandpa and Uncle Edwin did not unmask the arsonist it would leave the community devastated and in fear. Rumors spread attributing guilt to someone determined to settle a score. I could understand why someone would seek revenge and felt a bit elated at the thought Grandpa and Uncle Edwin were getting paid back! It was exactly what they deserved.

Grandpa was annoying and his duplicitous personality aggravated me. I felt little compassion or sorrow when he fell on hard times and always believed he got exactly what he merited. I remember how the sound of Grandpa's sing-song voice irritated me when he preached during Sunday service. It was the cause of much mockery and laughter among the children and young folk in the community.

When he preached, he had a particular ritual. He rose to his feet, walked around his chair, and paused directly behind it. Slowly he elevated his head, swaying it from side to side in steady circular movements. He then rolled his eyes several times before dropping his upper lids.

It seemed as if Grandpa was on a journey to a foreign world.

For a brief moment he was absent. Returning, he addressed the congregation in an alien voice, reserved exclusively for preaching, quoting scripture and speaking his mind in Church. He appeared to be in a trance. Often after the service, I joined the young folk in poking fun at him and his odd manner, pretending to be Grandpa, crooning in his ridiculous sing-song voice. I never felt guilty about anything I did against Grandpa because his conniving, hypocritical personality caused me such misery.

One Saturday evening, before drifting off to sleep, I overheard a conversation between Mom and Dad. Mom was usually talkative when not in Dad's company but had a tendency to maintain a respectful silence when he was present. This was a common practice among the Old Order Amish Community. Women were neither permitted to vote, nor render decisions and judgments. Instead they were "breeders," and totally submissive to their husbands and fathers.

"I had a meeting with the Preachers today," the Bishop said, "and we came to an agreement about how to punish Dad." He was talking about my Grandpa.

"Davie, what has your father done?" Mom said.

"Amelia, the 'English' man brought logs for Dad to cut into lumber. He filled the order but was dishonest and kept a bundle for himself.

"Dad was deceitful. He stole and I must punish him."

My heart raced with joy at the thought of Grandpa Burkholder getting punished. I wanted to know more. I wanted to see with my own eyes and fully enjoy the moment but I knew I would not be permitted.

Dad called a special meeting at Church which was open to members only. The Elders, Preachers and Deacons participated. Children and Young Folks under the age of eighteen were not considered members; therefore, their attendance was prohibited.

I was told that Grandpa knelt in front of the Bishop, Preachers and Deacons. Once in this submissive position he was urged to admit his wrong doing: A straightforward declaration of guilt. There is no defense for a misdeed and no justification; only an acknowledgement of sin and acceptance of punishment to rectify the wrong. The Bishop addressed Grandpa's sin and urged the members to forgive him, reminding them that Grandpa was "like a sheep that has gone astray."

"Are you prepared to confess your evil deed?" Dad said to Grandpa.

"Yes, I am," Grandpa said.

Grandpa's confession was witnessed by the Young Folks who gloated and snickered over his display of human frailty. He was scrutinized and, in front of everyone, whipped.

"I ask the forgiveness of Church and the Lord," Grandpa said. "I have done wrong."

The Bishop once again addressed the flock:

"If any member has reason not to forgive this man, let him come forward and speak his mind now." He then reminded them that, when the Lord was asked how many times to forgive a brother His response was, "I say to you not seven but seventy-seven times."

After several moments of silence the Bishop declared his father forgiven by Church and the Lord and raised him to his feet with a firm handshake and a full kiss on the lips. However, the humiliation left him bitter and contributed to his distancing himself from Dad and the rest of us. There were no more overnight visits and his words to Dad and his grandchildren were silenced. I cannot say that this separation disturbed me. Quite the contrary; I was delighted not to have to see Grandpa and be subjected to his brutal beatings. My memories of him were unpleasant and I shuddered whenever I thought about his two-faced personality and cold, calloused hand slapping my cheek. Still, I felt I had a score to settle: One day.

During my last months in Bowling Green, my behavior was often not in keeping with Dad's rules. However, that was OK as long as I got away with it.

I learned the answers to some of my questions and then questioned many of the answers. I was seldom satisfied with the explanations I received and often wondered why. I knew I was different even at seven years of age, but I did not know why.

I continued to watch Dad closely. He was my teacher. Sometimes I pulled away, especially when his brutal punishments did not make sense. I did not like his duplicitous nature and his "broken truth" aggravated me. I was confused and unable to put together the intricate puzzle growing in my mind. I had additional questions and wanted even more answers. I was determined to have them: The seed planted and fertilized was now beginning to bud.

❋ ❋ ❋

II

Maywood, Missouri

Fall of 1979–
Fall of 1983

CHAPTER 6

Dad had become embittered and distressed by the unprecedented turn of events occurring in Bowling Green. The prevalence of Amish drinking in the community and driving cars with the 'English' conflicted with his way of thinking. He feared these evil changes would influence his family in a harmful manner and felt it was time to leave Bowling Green and head for a new life in Maywood.

I was excited about moving and looking forward to a new adventure. The anticipation of having a new house in a new community was thrilling. I remember the morning Dad loaded the family into the van. Fired up with the enthusiasm of explorers embarking on a different journey we departed Bowling Green.

"Today is an important day," Dad said, as the van backed up and turned around to begin the ride. The crackling echo of tires crunching the gravel along the lane leading away from the farm bid a final goodbye.

"We're starting over. We're beginning a new life in a new community," Dad said.

"Where are we going, Dad?" I said.

"We're going on to Maywood, Christy," he said.

"Are we the only ones going?" I asked.

"No Christy, Dad replied, "There are two other families making the move."

"When will we get there?" I said.

I was unable to sit still. My heart was racing and the thought of a new house, new school and new friends was overpowering.

"We will be there soon," Dad said, "in an hour or so."

Elma and I played a game to pass the time. We turned our heads from side to side as we passed different farms and tried to pick out our new house.

"Dad, which house is ours? Is that it?" I asked, pointing to an old wood framed house to the left of the van.

"No, Christy," Dad said. "Be patient. We're not there yet."

We traveled for an hour on the highway, before the van turned on to a gravel road and continued at a steady pace. Sometimes I closed my eyes, picturing in my mind the new house, the barn and school I would attend. Suddenly my reverie was interrupted; I felt my spirits soar as I sat upright in my seat. Wide-eyed, I realized the van had climbed up and over a steep hill. The impact shook me back to reality.

"That's it!" Dad said as we turned into a lane leading to a house. "That's our new house!" I fixed my gaze on the house. I was eager to get out of the van and explore my new surroundings.

This was home. I loved it immediately and felt life would be different here. I was living a new beginning. There was a peaceful aura of stillness. A chorus of sparrows chirped a welcome as we pulled into the driveway. I was happy and excited. A subtle breeze greeted me as I stepped from the van. It rocked my hat and seemed to engage me in capricious play.

"Maywood will be a joyful change," I thought.

The house was a single story home topped with a dilapidated green roof that seemed to have exceeded its natural lifespan a decade ago. I moved closer, my eyes vigilantly surveying the exterior structure. My gaze focused on the basement. It had a walk out! This was different; Amish homes were not constructed in this manner. Usually the main door was the only available means for gaining entry or departing.

"Rebecca," I said jumping up and down "Did you see this! Come here quickly! Isn't this cool! We can actually get out of the basement through the walk out! We don't have to go up stairs. This is real cool! Nobody in Bowling Green had anything like this."

"Yeah, Christy," she said "This is great. I think it'll be fun living here!"

"I'm so proud of Dad," I said. "Can you believe he actually bought a house with a walk out basement? Rebecca, Dad is cool!"

The tractor trailers began unloading the cattle, chickens and other animals. Echoes of yelps, grinding gravel and jarring clip-clops shattered the quiet of nature. I sprinted down the path, unsettling the pebbles, giving life to clouds of sandy dust: I was in another world!

Once inside the house, Dad lifted the carpet covering the living room floor and pulled out the tiny nails holding it secure around the edges. He rose from his crouched position, stood a moment, drew a deep breath, then bent over and scrapped away the sticky traces of glue. Once the carpet was removed, I could see the old tongue and grove pine floor. Curious I went down on my knees and rubbed my hand along the notched pine. It was abrasive and scratchy. I knew it would probably splinter easily and I shuddered while remembering how it hurt the last time Mom yanked a sliver of wood from my foot.

There were two bedrooms in the house, each complete with linoleum flooring. This was a first. Linoleum flooring was prohibited in the Amish community.

"Rebecca," I said, "Look at this floor!"

"Christy, it feels smooth," she said, running her index finger along the slippery linoleum. "No splinters!"

"I wonder if Dad's gonna leave it," I said.

Rebecca looked at me and shrugged her shoulders.

Mom's cook stove was moved into the kitchen and the lanterns and oil lamps were unpacked and set out. Two men hoisted the gas wringer washing machine from the van and carried it down to the basement. I made endless trips to the van to remove our belongings. The machinery was unloaded in the barn, and the animals were settled in their stalls.

It was a memorable day; a day filled with the exhilaration of a new start.

This was home. I felt hopeful and elated. It was a new feeling and it put me in high spirits. Dad had mentioned during the journey that there would be some interesting changes. I think he told the truth again.

"Maybe Dad is changing also," I thought to myself.

I looked up at him with inquisitive eyes, eager to learn more about my new surroundings and my new life. So many questions were turning in my mind.

"Life will be better here," Dad said to Rebecca, Elma and me. "You'll enjoy living in Maywood. However, you still have to obey the rules."

I was delighted.

The first winter in Maywood was freezing and snowy. Rebecca, Elma, William and I slept in the attic in the same bedroom. The girls cuddled in a small bed, while William and I snuggled in a larger bed under several layers of blankets and a big heavy quilt. Every morning we awakened with our noses and the tips of our ears red and stinging from the bitter cold. We quivered and shivered, unable to speak. Our teeth chattered, puffs of smoke billowed from our mouths when we spoke and our bones rattled. The tiny drops of saliva forming on the edges of our tongues frosted. To warm up we ran downstairs and huddled in front of the wood stove, encircling our arms around its hot belly. Bright yellow sparks from the smoldering firewood gave illumination to the predawn darkness. A bucket Dad filled with drinking water the night before stood nearby. I noticed it was a solid block of ice. A heady fragrance infiltrated the room: It was musky and ambrosial, warm and inviting. It was the reassuring scent of home and hearth; soothing and comforting.

The first year, Rebecca, Elma and I were home schooled. Mom seated us in the living room every morning and continued the lessons we started in Bowling Green. I was relieved not to have to attend school. My recollections of the beatings I received at the hands of bullies still pained me. I cringed at the thought. Studying at home also freed me from the embarrassment and humiliation of being ridiculed and laughed at because I was short and pigeon-toed.

"Not being a victim is sure nice," I said to myself.

Many more families moved to Maywood the following spring. The Elders decided the children would attend school at Teacher Noah's house which was about three miles distant from ours.

Teacher Noah was a frail, middle-aged married man with a dark complexion and a somber facial expression. He wore wire framed glasses and a six inch beard. At a young age he suffered a crippling bout of polio which left him with one leg shorter than the other. This physical failing, however, did not render him useless. In the Old Order Amish Community, most of the teachers were either handicapped or nuns and teaching was a suitable way for them to earn a living since it did not involve physical agility or strength.

Every morning, Mom crammed our lunch pails with cold-packed hamburger sandwiches, apples, and some home-made cottage cheese. We took off swinging our stuffed lunch pails and headed down to Uncle Edwin's where we met cousins Edna and Ruben Burkholder. We then continued across the field to Uncle Ralph's to where my best friend Isaac and his brother James waited for us. Once all together we crossed the highway and proceeded down the gravel road for the remaining two mile run. It was exciting and I enjoyed my new life in Maywood.

Teacher Noah was very stern. His method was rigid and uncompromising. One day Isaac and I flew a paper airplane made from a sheet of note paper. We laughed and giggled as we threw it back and forth following its short smooth course with our eyes.

"Christy!" Teacher Noah said, "Come up here: Immediately!"

"You all know I do not allow laughing and carrying on in class. Christy, hand over that plane right now. Lay your hands on the desk palms down!"

Scared, I did as I was told. Teacher Noah took two hesitant steps forward then snatched the discolored wooden ruler he kept on his desk. It was his constant companion. He struck me three times across my knuckles with the notched edge. I drew in my breath, held it, shut my eyes and stood motionless. I knew that if I moved even to breathe he would repeat the punishment. Although I was caught red-handed I was still angry and upset with Teacher Noah's painful knuckle swatting. He humiliated me in front of the entire school for flying a paper airplane!

"I'll show him," I whispered to myself.

After school Isaac and I hurried out behind the barn to where Teacher Noah kept his pony.

"Hold the pony, Isaac," I said fired up.

"What are you going to do?" Isaac asked.

"Nothing. Just give him the same beating Teacher Noah gave me today," I said. "He has to pay for hurting me and embarrassing me in front of everyone."

I grabbed a stick and determined to get even; I slammed it across the pony's back three times. Frightened and in pain, he pushed back with his hind legs. Anticipating his reaction I jumped back, just in time to avoid a swift kick in the groin.

The children, hearing the loud swat of the stick hitting the pony's back bone, ran over in time to witness the whipping. They told Teacher Noah who in turn informed Dad. That evening I received another lashing with Dad's leather strap, my first in Maywood. I knew I deserved it.

"The next time I settle a score, I'll do it without getting caught," I promised myself.

Despite the lashing, my spirit was still high. I had every good intention of obeying Dad's rules even though I knew I would probably slip and break them from time to time. I loved my new life in Maywood, eager to be a part of exciting events and crucial happenings.

One Sunday when Church service was not scheduled the family reunited around the oak table to enjoy an unhurried lunch. Dad read passages from the Scriptures and explained the meaning and lessons to be learned, answering any questions we asked. Afterwards we sat around talking and reading books. Sunday was a day of rest.

"God blessed the seventh day and made it holy because on it He rested from all His work," Dad cited from Scriptures. "And He gave to man a commandment: Thou shalt keep holy the Lord's Day."

Later that afternoon Rebecca, Elma and I went out to the barn and up to the hay mow to play. I set up a milk stool, positioned myself on it and emulated Dad's preaching. Rebecca and Elma were amused and I was encouraged to continue. Soon tiring of this activity I suggested we play a different game.

"Rebecca, let's play cow," I said stepping down from the milk stool and kicking it out of my path.

"OK, Christy," she said.

I placed my open hand between her legs, right on her crotch and began moving my fingers. I pretended her genitals were a cow's udder. I groped, squeezed and stroked her, delighting myself while pleasing her. She seemed in tune with my rhythm and moved accordingly, giggling and laughing as I ran my fingers up and down her genitals.

Rebecca seemed to enjoy the game and I hoped she would keep her mouth shut and not tattle. I was dreaming as usual. That evening, before supper Rebecca approached Dad.

"Christy did a bad thing again today," she said in her sing-song voice. "He made me play cow and he touched me where he's not supposed to."

"Amelia, where is Christy?" Dad said.

"He's out in the wood shed, Davie," Mom said. "I asked him to get some logs to fill my wood box."

Dad rushed out to confront me.

"Christy, you behaved badly again today," he said. His tone was stern, though he remained composed and in control.

"Rebecca tells me you touched her inappropriately. I'm upset with you, Christy. You know it's wrong and you know it's a sin."

Dad grabbed one of the two foot long wood sticks that were

cut for lighting the kitchen stove. He gave me three swift lashings. They stung my back and I knew I would be sore and have trouble sitting for several days. Upset and humiliated, I thought of Rebecca.

"I don't like Rebecca at all," I said to myself. "That girl has the cunning of Satan. She's two faced and always scheming to get me in trouble with Dad." This time she was lucky and did not get whipped for allowing me to fondle her.

After my whipping in the wood shed, I felt disgusted and angry. I was confused and angry Rebecca had escaped her due punishment and wondered why Dad let her off the hook. I decided it would be wise to avoid her and use my time and energy to gain favor with Dad. I knew Dad held me accountable for my wrong doings; therefore I understood why my whippings were deserved. Bad things were sins and sins merited punishment.

I noticed Dad was in better spirits since our move to Maywood. He seemed to be different; repeating jokes he heard from the 'English,' whistling tunes as he went about completing his daily chores and singing songs at milking time. This was not the Dad I knew in Bowling Green. His morale was high and his outlook optimistic. He was a changed man. I liked the new Dad. His upbeat attitude was encouraging: Maybe it was contagious!

I forgave him for lying. The episode occurred such a long time ago and it was only one lie. I admired Dad's intelligence and recognized that his decision to move the family away from Bowling Green was smart. I was no longer obliged to be in the company of Grandpa Burkholder and Uncle Ben. The abuse at their hands was just a ghastly memory. I no longer feared Sundays and the brutal whippings I received from the mean boys who tormented me because I was the Bishop's son. I felt free. It was my first taste of freedom! It felt good! I liked it and I wanted more!

Dad seemed to be more light-hearted and forgiving and as the days passed I began to look at him with different eyes. He gained my approval and respect. I was proud of who he was: A man so powerful and so free. He was my hero!

I couldn't wait to grow up. I wondered how it would feel to

be totally liberated. My inquisitive mind questioned what I would do if I were free and more importantly when I was free. I vowed to find out someday.

I was happy. I had a hero. I had a goal. My one problem was my height. I was self-conscious and weary of being teased because I was short. If only I could grow a bit taller, life would be perfect. I had to find a way and realized my only hope was to turn to the Lord for help.

While feeding the cows, I'd look over my right shoulder then quickly swing my head over to the left to see if anyone was approaching. When I was certain the coast was clear, I'd duck down behind the manger, kneel down and pray.

"Lord, please make me a little taller. If you let me grow I promise I will never do bad things again. I won't disobey Dad or touch Rebecca and Elma inappropriately again. Please, Lord, I need to be taller."

If all else fails, turn to the Lord: Prayer works. Later I would have the confirmation.

❋   ❋   ❋

Chapter 7

Life in Maywood was full of pleasant experiences. To a nine year old boy, it was a time of learning, investigating and questioning. My mind was becoming more open and accepting of the new thoughts and feelings rising within; thoughts and feelings that would eventually materialize and surface. I lived, walking in the heel marks Dad left behind, fascinated by his power and attracted to the freedom he earned.

Dad never failed to surprise me. One day after attending a public auction, he returned home excited. He stuck his head in the door.

"Amelia! Christy! Come out to the porch!" he said. "I've got something I'd like to show you." At the sound of Dad's voice, I ran past Mom, knocked into Rebecca and dashed out on the porch.

"Christy," Dad said, "Take a look at this!"

I lowered my glance and noticed a blue Home Lite chain saw. My mouth dropped open. I was shocked!

"Dad, this is a chain saw!" I said excited. I bent over to touch it. I had to be certain it was real.

In the Old Order Amish Community in Bowling Green, it was forbidden to own a chain saw. Even to touch one that belonged to an 'English' man was prohibited. There were rumors that some of the Amish had run a neighbor's chain saw and were severely punished for "breaking the rules." I was astonished and overwhelmed.

"Dad is really powerful!" I said to Rebecca. "Look at the cool chain saw he bought."

I was fascinated by this new piece of machinery and had to learn how to operate it. I picked it up, turned it around, rolled the chain and looked it over.

"Dad," I said, "it has a trigger!"

"Yes, Christy," Dad said, "pulling the trigger makes the motor speed up." It was too cool. I decided that one day I would have my own chain saw. This was an unforgettable day, and marked the start of many exciting moments I would enjoy in Maywood.

I have fond memories of my second Christmas in the new community. It was early winter in 1981 and I had begged Dad for a BB gun not daring to believe I would receive one.

"Dad," I said, "could I have a BB gun? If I had one I could kill the rats and mice running around the hog house."

"We'll see, Christy," Dad replied, changing the subject.

During the holidays we never had a Christmas tree to decorate or place gifts under. Instead, Mom hung up a dark curtain to close off the entry way between the kitchen and living room.

"No peeking behind the curtain," Mom said, "until Dad and I awaken tomorrow morning." We all shook our heads in agreement, too excited to protest.

It was Christmas Eve and in keeping with tradition, we each set a place for ourselves at the table before retiring for the evening. The following morning when I came down to breakfast my eyes darted around the table stopping at my place. I was eager to see what I would find. There in front of my plate, taking up an entire corner of the table, was a big BB gun!

"The BB gun," I shouted breathlessly, "Dad got me the BB gun! Mom, Rebecca, Elma, come look at my BB gun!" I was so proud, I was delirious with joy!

One day while Dad was mowing and I was hard at work hoeing the thistles that grew in the pasture my gaze suddenly settled on a Billy goat. He was struggling and seemed to be in distress. I ran over just in time to rescue the animal. His head was trapped between two wires in the fence and he was pulling and twisting his body to get out. The Billy goat belonged to one of our neighbors, Rob Goodin, an 'English' man. Mr. Goodin's house was situated about three quarters of a mile west of ours and held a special fascination for me. I was interested to gain entry, knowing he had electricity and other modern conveniences. The temptation was irresistible; overwhelming for a curious mind in search of answers.

Rob Goodin was out back running his lawn mower, when I approached him.

"Mr. Goodin, Mr. Goodin," I shouted, breathless. "One of your Billy goats had his head trapped in the fence. He was squirming and wiggling, trying to get out!"

Mr. Goodin immediately shut down his mower.

"Show me where he is, Chris, and I'll go free him right now."

"It's OK, Mr. Goodin," I said, "I already pulled his head out."

"Well, thanks a lot, Chris," Mr Goodin said smiling. "I appreciate your quick actions. When I see your father, I'll tell him what a fine son he has raised."

"The 'English' are really nice people," I thought to myself. I was disappointed I could not see his house but determined to get inside one day. Pleased with myself, I hurried back home not wanting Dad to notice I was gone for such a lengthy period of time.

A week later, Rob Goodin approached Dad.

"David," he said, "I'm leaving tomorrow. I'm going on a business trip and I'll be away for a while. Will you feed my cat and the goats in my absence?"

"Sure, Rob," Dad said. "Don't worry, I'll have Christy take care of it."

"Thanks, David," Rob said. "That son of yours is a good boy."

The 'English' did not use our Amish names and called us Chris and David instead of Christy and Davie. This always pleased me as I hated to be called Christy.

I noticed the corners of Dad's lips turned slightly upwards. I could see he was proud and enjoyed the compliment.

The following day, Rebecca and I ran down through the field and over to Rob Goodin's house to feed his animals.

I stepped up on the porch.

"Rebecca, I'm going to open the door," I said.

"Why Christy?" she said.

"'Cause I want to see the inside of the 'English' man's house," I said. "Come on, Rebecca, let me get a peek. Aren't you curious?"

"OK, Christy," she said, as I yanked open the door.

"Wow, Rebecca," I said, catching my breath. My eyes roamed over the interior of his living room.

"Look at all those evil things, Rebecca," I said pointing my finger at his TV. "Mr. Goodin has a TV, a radio and a telephone!"

"We must not stand here and look at those things," Rebecca said. "Dad says they are bad things. Let's go Christy." Although I was puzzled because I did not understand why the 'English' man had these sinful objects, I was curious and interested in learning more. That day, only a fear of the Lord impeded me from entering and touching Rob Goodin's evil possessions.

❋ ❋ ❋

The creek always intrigued me. It was a fun place to play and the gurgling waters were cooling during the torrid Maywood summers. One Sunday afternoon while playing along the creek with my cousins Isaac and James, I stripped off my clothes. They followed and we jumped into the water naked. While we swam we kept our eyes open for snakes which were often seen in the area.

"Christy, look! There's a snake crawling over there," Isaac said rising to his feet. He pointed to a long green and black snake crawling near the creek. It glimmered in the sunlight as it wiggled along its course.

I ran out of the water. Isaac and James followed me as I gave it a good chase. We were excited, and totally unconcerned about our naked bodies. Dad always said snakes were evil, therefore, if we caught one, we would swat it with a stick, to crush its head.

"Isaac," I said. "I think I got this one. Come here and take a look."

James watched as I turned the snake on its back and poked it in the belly. Giving it a quick look, he soon lost interest in the dead snake.

Afterwards, Isaac and I stood naked in the ankle deep water, flinging mud at each other.

"Christy," Isaac said, "Do you want to play James's game?"

Before I could respond, he positioned himself directly in front of me, took my hand and placed it on his penis.

"Now rub it, Christy," he said. "Rub it hard and fast; move it up and down. Like this." He put his cold muddy hand over my penis, tightened his grip and moved it up and down without pause.

I returned the favor, making a fist around his penis. After the shared pleasure, we continued hurling mud at some frogs who had settled near the creek.

On my way to the house I thought about this new explosive feeling in my groin. I knew it was definitely worth exploring. It was certainly more exciting than just flashing our penises at the girls whenever they were bold enough to disobey the rules by coming down to the creek to watch the boys swim.

❈   ❈   ❈

Dad moved the family from Bowling Green because he feared the turn of events: The drinking and wild behavior upset him. Fearful of the rowdy actions and prevailing rebellious attitude, he no longer desired any association with the Amish from that community.

Barn raisings were events organized to gather men from various communities for diverse initiatives. Usually they helped build new farm structures and mend properties that had suffered ruin from snow and lightning storms. These barn frolics were a vital part of the Old Order Amish Tradition. They were an occasion to integrate work projects with social events. The women prepared food and spent the day exchanging news and discussing the latest gossip while the men labored to complete the chores they had set out to do.

One Sunday, John Mast, a bald middle-aged Elder with a comical sense of humor, announced that Bowling Green Amish were coming for the barn raising at his farm. Dad, disapproving of their disruptive manner, was somewhat leery and disturbed by the event.

"The wild Bowling Green bunch is coming to Mast's barn raising," he said to Mom the evening before the event. His face was taut. A furrowed brow betrayed his concern.

The following day I arrived at John Mast's with Dad and was excited to see a green truck pull into the driveway. It was badly dented and dust laden. The truck was crammed with Bowling Green Amish, standing in the rear, yelling and carousing. Initially, the rowdy behavior intrigued me. Later, I was relieved to learn they were just visiting for the day.

"These wild people have fallen into sin," Dad told us. "They drink and drive the 'English' man's cars."

Listening to the ruckus they were making I was happy to be in Maywood.

"Dad was so smart to leave," I said to myself, thinking about my days in Bowling Green.

My memories of Bowling Green were painful. Remembering, I shuddered, swallowing hard to release the lump lodged in my throat! I would never forget those years. They were despicable. Yet, they were important and played a major role in reshaping my life.

The Amish always avoided purchasing new lumber. Instead when they needed it for projects, the men tore down old homes and buildings in the community and in neighboring towns. After collecting the lumber, they loaded it on to the trucks and brought it back. The boards were filled with old rusted nails that jutted from the surface. If not handled carefully, it was easy to pierce the skin on hands and fingers, sometimes drawing blood.

There was a huge lumber pile for the boys to clean up, at John Mast's barn raising. The procedure involved two teams. The first team of boys lined up in long rows and waited for the second team to carry over the pieces of lumber. Three boys worked on each board. They lifted it, flipped it over and examined the surface for bulging nails. The nails were hammered back then pulled out. A fourth boy gathered the smooth boards and stacked them. Once the boards were nail free, the men came down, took the clean lumber, cut it and fitted it to their needs.

I watched for awhile then shot a last quick glance at the boys hammering and pulling nails. They were drenched with sweat; their hands and fingernails black from handling the grimy boards. In search of a new adventure, I headed up to the barn, where the men were working with the chain saws, cutting and fitting the lumber.

"This is more like it," I said to myself as I walked over to the chain saw. I picked up a board and without hesitating, sawed it in half. I looked down at the two pieces of wood. I had cut my first piece of lumber! My heart was racing. I was actually building instead of just cleaning boards and pulling nails!

John Mast gave me the thumbs up.

"Good job, Christy. Those pieces of lumber look mighty good!" He said shouting in order to be heard above the ruckus.

I was proud of my accomplishment and thrilled to receive John's compliment.

Dad was working at the far end of the building. I noticed he paused to wipe the sweat from his brow. He spotted me and walked over to where I was standing.

"What are you doing, Christy?" Dad said. Not waiting for a response he continued, "Instead of hanging around go down to the lumber pile and help the others pull nails from the boards. Don't you know idleness is the devil's workshop? Now quick, move along. There's plenty of work to be done. You hear me, Christy?"

"Yes, Dad," I said, not knowing what question I was answering. I walked over to the lumber pile, about 200 feet from the hog house. Isaac was hard at work pulling nails. I helped him for a brief spell then tired of the monotonous task.

"Isaac," I said, "let's go check on the hogs."

"OK, Christy," he said, happy to get away.

John had built a concrete embankment with a surging spring directly in front of the hog troth. A rhythmic trickling sound greeted us as we arrived.

"Isaac," I said, "let's cool our feet in the water."

We sat along the side of the spring and dangled our feet, enjoying the soothing effect of the rippling water flowing between our toes. The pleasure was short lived.

"Christy," Dad said walking over with Uncle Ralph keeping pace, "what are you and Isaac doing down here in the hog house? I'll tell you what's going on. You boys are acting lazy and wasting time! Christy, I told you before and I'm going to tell you one more time; I don't approve of idleness. Now stand up!"

When we got to out feet Isaac and I each received two swift smacks across the face. Dad's hand was dirty, calloused and sweaty. It hurt!

"Get back to the lumber pile right now," Dad said, "and get to work." Not having another option, we returned to the boring task of nail pulling.

Somehow the slaps and smacks did little to curb my mischievous behavior; I continued "breaking Dad's rules."

Even painful consequences did not stop me from seeking new adventures: Some lessons were never learned. Often I ran over to the trash pile down the road. It was situated on a property that had been gutted and renovated; therefore there were many fascinating treasures to be found. William and I liked to search through the discarded items until we found something interesting. We took whatever we thought was worth having for ourselves.

One afternoon, while rummaging through a heap of trash I found a plastic water pistol.

"William," I said, "take a look at what I found. It's a water pistol! Isn't that cool?"

"Yeah, Christy," William said. "But doesn't Dad forbid us to have any kind of pistols? He always says they're dangerous!"

"No, William," I said, putting the gun in his hand. "This one's not dangerous. It's just a plastic water pistol." William looked at the pistol in his hand and turned it over twice to inspect the trigger.

"OK, Christy," he said handing it back. He seemed appeased by my words. I took the pistol from his hand, shoved it into my trouser pocket and later hid it in my room. I knew that if Dad found it I would get a whipping.

One Sunday afternoon while playing outside with William, I convinced him to help me fill the water pistol.

"William," I said, "help me fill the pistol. Unscrew the cap and hold the pistol steady."

I went over to the gas jug and poured gasoline into the gun. The odor was strong and offensive.

"Hold it steady, William," I said. "If you move the gas will drip out."

"Christy, my throat burns," he said.

"OK, William, I'm done. Give me the pistol." With the pistol in my hand, I squirted several times against the side of the house.

"William, I need some matches," I said. Let's go inside and get some."

I snuck into the kitchen and quietly walked over to the bucket of drinking water. I scooped out a glass and took a drink, offering some to William. Through the corner of my eyes I spotted Mom's matches on the counter. I snatched a handful, stuffed them in my pocket and ran back outside.

"William," I said, "stand here in front of me and light a match. I'm going to shoot through the flame. This'll be real cool. You'll see."

"OK, Christy," William said and promptly obeyed. I shot

several times. The tiny sparks that flew about every time I squirted did not satisfy my quest for adventure.

"William," I said, "Give me the matches."

I lit a match and slowly dangled it in front of the pistol careful not to let my hand movement extinguish it. I took a deep breath. The aroma of sulfur tickled my nose. Fighting a sneeze, I pulled the trigger. I was not ready for the explosion that followed. Frightened by the sudden swish and intensity of the billowing flames shooting up, William stepped back and fell to the ground.

"Christy's on fire!" he shouted.

I raced to the house. A raging fire was crawling along the sleeve of my shirt. It was scorching. I was gasping, choking and crying. I was terrified!

"Mom! Mom!" I screamed, "My arm's on fire! I'm burning!"

Mom jumped to her feet, ran over to the water bowl and pumped enough water to fill it to the brim. With quick movements she threw the water on my arm. It splashed my face and ran down the side of my shirt, extinguishing the fire.

"Christy, what have you done?" Mom said, once the flames were out. "You could have burned to death."

I knew I had done wrong. I also knew I would get a severe lashing before supper, but was relieved Mom had put the fire out before I burned to death.

That evening, after Dad was informed about my latest misadventure, he delivered four brutal lashings to my back. The pain was agonizing. I was, however, too happy to be alive to care.

❆   ❆   ❆

Chapter 8

Maywood was a time of happy memories and defining changes, but as I matured I began to feel as if something was not quite right. It was 1982 and at ten years of age my thoughts took me down many unexplored paths. I began to study Dad more closely. His contradictory behavior as the powerful Bishop in the community often confused and disturbed me. In the Old Order Amish Tradition, the Bishop was the supreme authority. His word was law. He judged his family and his flock and he condemned all who were found guilty of misdeeds.

To be held accountable to Dad and Church for my thoughts and actions irritated me. I began to find the harsh controls objectionable and wondered if I would be able to continue accepting his rule: And if so, for how much longer? Change was good; it meant I was growing and learning. However, change also seeded new controversies and conflicts: In school, at home and in Church.

In Maywood, school was taught by Teacher Noah. He was in a quandary over school being conducted in his house, believing the presence of children had become an intrusion on his family life. The issue was brought to the attention of the Elders who convened to discuss and resolve the matter. They decided to rent an abandoned house in Emerson; a small town populated with about twenty-five families. The property was designated as the new school. We were thrilled to be able to attend classes in a town and excited to be among the 'English.' I admired Dad for trusting me and my sisters and for allowing us to study in an Emerson school.

Teacher Noah was a rigid disciplinarian, never shy about imposing strong punitive measures.

"The 'English' will be driving along the road," he said at the start of class. He then grabbed his wood ruler, slammed it hard on the desk and continued, "anyone who is distracted, or rises to look out the window when a car passes will receive several swats across the knuckles. Is that clear?"

He emphasized the threat with another slam of the ruler.

"Yes, Teacher," the children said in unison.

I looked around the room to catch a glimpse of the children present. My glance fell on Anna Miller. She was the most beautiful girl I had ever seen. With her golden hair and flirty blues eyes she immediately captured my heart. Whenever she looked my way a spine tingling jolt made my face blush a bright crimson. I experienced my first crush!

It was early winter and the temperature had fallen the previous evening. Mom and Dad took the buggy into town to buy butter and eggs because the chickens were not always productive during cold spells. I was in the house with a slight fever, having defied Mom's order to wear shoes to school. The Amish usually walked barefoot, until the first frost covered the gravel roads. I, however, always enjoyed taking the opportunity to shuffle my bare feet in the soft fresh snow and had walked to school without my shoes. My defiant behavior was greeted with a throbbing headache, a stuffed, runny nose and a slap across the face. Bored with staying indoors to deal with my annoying cold I wanted to go outside and do something exciting.

"William," I said, "let's go tail-tying. Mom and Dad went to town so they won't know anything."

"What is tail-tying?" William said. "A new game?" Isaac and I did this a lot, but for William it would be a new adventure.

"Come with me to the barn and I'll show you," I said.

William and I headed for the shop and took a short rope. We ran over to the barn and up the silo. I grabbed some silage and headed out to where the cows were herding after feeding.

"William," I said, "hand me the rope."

"What for?" William said.

"Shh, William. Be quiet. Just do as I say and don't ask so many questions."

"OK, Christy," William said, "there's no need to get mad."

"I'm not mad," I said, "but you're sure annoying sometimes."

Dangling the silage in front of the cows' mouths, I managed to coax two of them into the barn. One was rather large, the other somewhat smaller. I lined them up with their butts facing each other. I took the rope and made two loops, one in each end. I slipped a noose around each tail and tightened it. The cows were now joined by their tails. I gave each cow a swat on the back. Both animals moved forward, and attempted to leave the barn through a narrow door. They ripped splinters of wood from the wall as they squeezed together to pass through the narrow opening. Once outside, William and I cheered them on, encouraging them to run. After the "pull off" in which each cow headed in an opposite direction, I noticed that the larger cow had severed the smaller cow's tail. It was dragging on the ground, bloody and covered with dirt, still attached to the noose. The little cow was tailless, bleeding, bucking and running around in pain. I did not expect this drastic outcome and felt my heart race.

I ran down the pasture to catch the large cow. I had to retrieve the tail!

"Christy," William said, "what're you going to do now? One cow has no tail and the other cow has two! Dad will give you a whipping."

I tried again to run after the large cow, but she got away. Frustrated, I gave up and returned to the house.

At milking time, Dad noticed the large cow, dragging the bloody tail.

"Christy," he said stunned," how did this happen? I want an answer now! Do you hear me?"

"Dad," I said, "William and I were just playing. We didn't mean to hurt the cows. I tried to catch the big one, but she got away."

"Christy," Dad said, "do you realize what you've done? Bend over now! Maybe this will make you understand what a bad thing you have done!"

He punished me for being a trouble maker, lashing me with the stick he used to discipline the cattle. William, who was only six years old, got off with one of Dad's calloused hand slaps. Although the smack stung his cheek, it was less painful than the beatings! Dad was unswerving in his sentencing. Once exposed for having committed a bad deed there was no reprieve from corporal punishment.

One evening, Rebecca, Elma and I suddenly noticed Dad's unusual and mysterious behavior. He was always consistent in his actions; therefore any deviation from his routine usually signified a serious matter. After supper he hitched Red up to the buggy, left in silence and returned rather late in the evening. He repeated this routine several times. It seemed to become a pattern.

"Where do you think Dad goes?" I said to Rebecca one evening shortly after supper.

"I don't know. Let's ask Mom," she said, heading over to the basin where Mom was rinsing the plates and dining utensils.

"Mom," I said, "where does Dad go every evening?"

"I don't know, Christy," she said, "I'm certain he'll tell us soon; just be patient."

I went to sleep without solving the mystery.

The following morning Mom prepared breakfast as usual. We began each day with coffee soup. To make this concoction she boiled a gallon of milk to which she added a half cup of Folgers coffee and two cups of sugar. Once brewed, she poured the mixture into a mixing bowl and blended it together with a loaf of stale bread cut into pieces. The coffee soup was hot and mushy and tasted syrupy. After adding fried potatoes to the soup we boisterously slurped it down, with neither concern nor attention to table manners. Good manners were a non-existent issue in the

Amish Tradition and the disturbing sounds of rude dining habits, belches and passing gas were not scorned.

One morning, just before leaving the breakfast table, Dad cleared his throat.

"I've been visiting with the Amish people who settled three miles from here at the far end of the community," he said. "There are five families." He paused a moment, drew a deep breath, stretched his arm and took a drink of water. His facial expression was somber. Dad's eyes were downcast; his brow more creased than usual. I knew something serious was bothering him.

"There are Amish people in the community who are doing bad things," he said shaking his head. "They're driving the 'English' man's cars! I visited with them and discussed their sinful behavior, but they paid no attention. They defied my warning."

I felt a knot in my stomach. Amish people were driving cars!

"Dad," I said, "don't they know they will go to hell?"

"Yes, Christy, they know they're condemned!" Dad said.

"Then why are they doing it, if they know they'll go to hell?"

"Christy, these are weak people, who have fallen into temptation. They have sinned against the Lord," he said. "If any of you see an Amish driving a car, turn away. Do you hear me?"

"Yes, Dad," we responded.

"Do not speak with these people and when they pass by do not look at them. They are evil people who are doing shameful things. They have "broken the rules." They have angered the Lord. They are condemned!"

Dad rose from the table, visibly distressed. It was quite a change from his usual calm and unruffled demeanor.

Scared by the thought of bad people invading the community, I picked up my lunch pail and ran the three miles to school. I was upset and could not erase Dad's words from my mind. At school I settled myself and waited for the lessons to begin.

Suddenly I heard a choking, thumping sound. Gazing out the window I noticed a big old black car come to a halt in front of the school. It was a 60s model coup, driven by Toby Miller. In the rear sat Anna, the girl I had a crush on, and her two brothers. Their dad had driven them to school! I jumped to my feet along with the other children to get a better look. How strange it was to see a car instead of a buggy outside the school and how sad to think Anna and her family would be damned to hell. I shuddered, trying to shake the disturbing thought.

"Get back to your seats," Teacher Noah said, slamming his ruler on the desk. "We're here to learn, not to stare out the window! Open your books and continue reading, while I step outside a moment," he said walking over to the door and pulling it open.

I immediately left my seat along with several other curious children and ran to the window just in time to see Teacher Noah approach Toby Miller. The two men began to converse. The sharp tones of their loud voices and laughter penetrated the walls of the school house.

"Isaac," I said. "This is scary. Do you think Teacher Noah is one of the bad people?"

"I don't know, Christy," Isaac said, "but he's sure carrying on with Mr. Miller, laughing and talking."

My thought was interrupted by the entry of Anna and her brothers. They came in silently and walked over to their desks. It was evident by their tense facial expressions and downcast eyes that they were nervous and anxious. I looked at Isaac who had his gaze fixed on Anna and her brothers.

"Isaac," I said, shaking his arm to break the stare. "Stop staring at them. I wonder how they will look when they go to hell!"

In my mind I tried to picture Anna and her brothers burning in hell. A chill ran up and down my spine as tiny beads of sweat formed on my forehead. It was a terrifying thought. I could not imagine the girl I had a crush on going to hell. Once Anna and her brothers were inside the school, Teacher Noah returned as quickly as he had departed and the lessons resumed. He behaved as if nothing had occurred.

On the following Sunday, Anna and her family were present in Church. Several Preachers and a Bishop from a neighboring community were also in attendance. Although they were unaware at the onset of the service, the Miller's, the other Bishop in our community and additional individuals who had sinned were to be condemned in front of the congregation. Several families were absent, unwilling to face their damnation. It was a rare occurrence to have two Bishops presiding in the same community.

After Church service, a special meeting was convened to discuss the evil doings in the community. I was out in the barn since, at ten years of age, I was not old enough to attend.

In the Amish tradition, those who departed Church early were the damned: The evil people who had "broken the rules." Once they left it was unlikely they would return.

From where I sat in the barn I was able to watch many of the Amish exit Church, hitch up their horses and return to their homes. Six families had been condemned. I saw the Miller's walk out, jump into their buggies and drive off. Even the Bishop from the far end of the community had been condemned. Dad stood alone with the four remaining families.

I was troubled and confused. With a burdened heart I repeated over and over in my mind the questions that plagued me. I searched desperately for answers, not yet knowing it would take a little more time and a lot more pain and suffering before I would be able to discover the whole truth and free my mind from the many frightful unknowns.

That evening I tossed and turned, unable to settle my spirit, and put my mind to rest. The questions continued churning.

"Aren't these individuals children of God? Weren't they created in His image and likeness? Don't they walk in the footsteps of the Lord just like Dad and the rest of the Amish people? How could they drift away? How could they lose favor with the Lord and be condemned to hell? Why did the Lord let this happen?"

I was frustrated, upset and baffled. I was in over my head and could not understand how these Amish people could betray the Lord. Why would they choose to burn in hell! Of all people how could an Amish Bishop, considered the holiest of men go to hell?

The following morning during breakfast I sought some answers.

"Dad," I said, "why are those people going to hell?"

"Christy," Dad said, "they're driving cars. They have contradicted and defied the Amish rules. They chose to follow the 'English' man's path to damnation and with him they will perish in the burning fires of hell. Remember, Christy, the 'English' man is not a child of the Lord. He is a sinner and his behavior should not be imitated. Do you understand what I'm saying?"

"Yes Dad," I said even though I was still confused and plagued by so many still unanswered questions.

I wondered how many more people would be going to hell!

After the departure of the six Amish families who were condemned and ostracized for choosing to follow the modern ways of the 'English' man, Dad decided we would no longer attend school in Emerson. He moved the school to a building on our property and built a room for the teacher who had arrived from another Amish community. Life in Maywood was beginning to resemble Bowling Green and although I had tried to be less mischievous, once again I was getting into trouble and facing Dad's punishments.

There was no reprieve for wrong doings: The score was always settled.

Chapter 9

Another year passed. It was 1983 and I settled into Maywood, enjoying my days as an eleven year old boy, eager to explore and learn about life. Many conflicts and contradictions arose with each new experience I lived. It was easier to "break the rules" and I began to question the validity of certain practices and procedures, that Dad preached in Church on Sundays and at home. Temptations were abundant and seemed more enticing than usual. Sometimes both the force and the will to overcome were either unconsciously missing or willfully rejected. Often my disagreements with Dad and the Elders led to anger, frustration and continued acts of retribution. Violence made me feel avenged in the face of a wrong doing at my expense. However, as a result a powerful inner chaos boiled to the surface, bothering me, confusing me and causing me to withdraw.

I knew I felt different. I knew I wanted more: But I didn't yet know why I was so unlike the others, what exactly I wanted and how I would get it. I knew I had a distressing dilemma to resolve and a mountain of questions to ask; questions for which I did not yet have answers.

This was a time of many new beginnings and numerous firsts. I was growing up and forced to deal with the issues born of a developing body as well as a budding mind.

Isaac and James often spent the night with us when their dad, Uncle Ralph and his wife were away from the community. Our house had two bedrooms on the second floor; one for Mom and Dad and the other for the children. Since James had a reputation for being an unruly and disruptive boy Dad thought it best to separate the boys from the girls. He settled me, William, James and Isaac in a room on the ground floor of the house. The bed was far too small to accommodate four boys and we were crammed together, barely able to breathe.

Isaac and I bragged a bit about some of the naughty things we had done. William and James chuckled and we felt even prouder.

After the small talk and laughter, everyone quieted down. Suddenly I felt a hand on my shoulder.

"Christy, turn on your side and hold still," James whispered. "You're gonna enjoy this."

Before I could respond, James took out his penis and tried to stick it in my butt.

"James, stop it," I groaned. "That's annoying! What're you doing?"

He laughed; a laugh that was more like a lusty snicker than an amused chuckle.

"Christy, if you relax and hold still and let me get in there, you'll get a thrill," James said and lunged into me one more time. He was panting and sweating. His body odor was intense; more pungent and foul than usual.

"No, stop it, James!" I said, jumping up from my submissive position on the bed. "This is a bad thing you're doing. If you do it one more time I'm going to tell Dad! Do you hear me James? Now, quit it!"

Understanding I was serious, James rolled over on to his other side.

"Isaac," he said, "Christy is a big baby. He's no fun at all! I just want to have some fun. Let me play with you. OK, Isaac?"

"No, James," Isaac said, "mind your own business."

"You're just two big babies," James said, exhaling. His warm breath hit my face. It was nasty and smelled as if he had sneaked a few puffs on a cigarette. Then he flipped over and went to sleep, frustrated and dissatisfied.

The following day we amused ourselves out in the barn. Isaac and I were standing together chatting when James walked over.

"Let's free the calves in the bottle pen," he said.

"Why James?" I asked.

"'Cause I want to play a game," he said grinning. "You'll see. It'll be fun."

Taking his suggestion, we went over to the pen and let the calves loose in the loafing shed. They seemed happy to be able to walk around and grunted their delight, one at a time.

Suddenly James extended his arm and grabbed a small rope hanging in the milking parlor which was used to contain the cows during milking. The rope which substituted the chain hobbles was fastened to their hind legs to prevent them from bucking. It was a less abrasive technique and did not cause painful flesh wounds especially on the cows that were agitated and uncooperative during milking. These capricious animals needed to be restrained on an almost daily basis.

"Christy, Isaac, don't just stand there," James said swinging the rope in circles above his head; "Help me catch a calf."

"What for, James?" I said.

"You'll see. Just help me get one."

We caught a calf and James tied it to the bunk. "Now the fun starts," James said laughing.

He unbuttoned his pants and dropped them to the ground along with his underwear. With a quick motion he lunged into the calf's backside. Penetrating the animal he started thrusting, accelerating his pace with every lunge. His breathing was heavy and his face flushed. It was obvious he was aroused.

"Christy, Isaac," he said breathless, "Come over here. It's your turn. This is a lot of fun. Try it. You'll see."

"No, James," I said. "I don't want to do that to the calf." "Me neither," Isaac said.

"You two are babies," James said poking fun at Isaac and me. "You're chicken shits; just plain old chicken shits."

He picked up his trousers, fumbled nervously with the buttons, retrieved his hat from the ground, dusted it off with a brusque tap of the hand, placed it on his head and walked away.

James was quite a naughty boy, with a ravenous appetite for sexual experimentation and gratification. He talked about it, he went in search of it and he tried to convince Isaac and me to be accomplices to his wild acts. He struggled to get us to participate in his antics, knowing he'd obtain additional pleasure as a spectator. When we denied his wishes he became upset and mean spirited. He cursed, mocked us and fired insults in a desperate attempt to intimidate us into obeying his demands.

The following Sunday, Isaac, James, my bushy blond haired cousin Rubin and I went for a walk behind the barn and down to the creek. Once there, we hurled rocks into the murky water. The impact of the rocks hitting the rippling water created a series of splashing thuds, interrupting the early morning silence.

On our return to the barn James walked ahead, taking several quick steps. He passed Isaac, Rubin and me. Once there was a suitable distance between us, he abruptly turned to face us.

"Christy, Rubin," James said. "I've got something to show you. This is fun and it will make you feel good!"

James undid the buttons on his pants. They slid immediately to his ankles. He yanked down his underwear.

"Isaac, come over here," he said, "pull your pants down." Isaac followed his older brother's orders. He dropped his pants and stood in front of us in his underwear and shirt. His gaze was fixed on his feet.

"Isaac, you know you have to take off your underwear. How can I play with you if you're all covered up?"

Isaac again heeded his brother's command and removed his underwear.

As soon as Isaac was in position, James mounted him, forcing his penis into the young boy's butt. Laughing and gasping for air he continued to plunge and thrust until he climaxed. Isaac grimaced and moaned. I was standing nearby and could see the act was painful. A gush of warm blood rushed to my face. Rubin, who was by nature a timid, retiring boy, shut his eyes. His complexion took on a scarlet hue in response to James's antics. Witnessing James in the throes of anal sex with Isaac made us feel uncomfortable and disgusted. It was embarrassing.

I glanced over at Rubin who stood shuffling his feet in the dirt. His head was bowed and his silence conveyed his disapproval.

"James," I said, "you did a bad thing to Isaac. You're going to get in trouble for this. If your dad finds out you'll both get a whipping."

"No, Christy," James said, "Isaac and I do this all the time. We never get caught."

"Rubin," I said, "let's go back to the barn. James is doing evil things. He's bad. One day he's going to get punished. This is big trouble. I don't want to get caught with him. Hurry, let's get out of here. Come on, Rubin, let's run. I want to get back to the barn before Dad or Uncle Ralph find out."

James was an insatiable exhibitionist. His sexual activities were not satisfying unless he had an audience to witness his actions. Sometimes it seemed as if my presence stimulated his appetite. One afternoon while Isaac, James and I enjoyed a swim in the creek, he again mounted Isaac and performed anal sex under the gurgling water with me as an unwilling observer.

James' reckless behavior was lewd and offensive. I thought he was excessively bad and was bothered by the manner in which in treated Isaac. His acts were selfish and performed with little regard for his victims. I felt uneasy and mortified to be a part of his lustful activities. My stomach was tied in knots and I fought a strong feeling of recurring nausea. I was confused and did not understand his repeated quest for sexual gratification in front of others.

A week later while putting up hay at Uncle Ralph's, James and I went over to the barn while the men convened under a big shady oak tree. The men always gathered during lunch break to relax, exchange jokes and stories and discuss the morning's events.

James and I noticed my younger sister Jenny, playing in the barn with Cousin Ellie, James and Isaac's sister. Jenny was Mom and Dad's sixth child, born December 16, 1977. Both girls were laughing and chatting animatedly. Their childish giggles echoed delightfully creating a happy environment. They seemed to be lighthearted and enjoying each other's company.

"Jenny," James said, interrupting their fun, "go up to the house; your mom's waiting for you."

Puzzled, Jenny glanced at Ellie who smiled in agreement. Satisfied, she obeyed her cousin's command, picked up her dolls and hurried away.

Meanwhile, I went to take a poop in the horse stall. Usually when nature dictated a need, it was preferable to just go in the barn instead of heading to the outhouse.

"Christy," James said, after directing Ellie to settle herself in the rear of the barn, "come back when you're done pooping, I've got something to show you. This will be more fun than the game I played with Isaac and the calves."

I was unable to imagine what James was planning, but being curious I quickly buttoned my pants, left the horse stall and ran to the back of the barn to see for myself.

"Ellie," James said, pointing to the hay rack "hurry! Go lay down under there."

With a flirty smile and aware of what was about to take place, she removed her underwear, walked over to the parked hay rack, got down on her knees, slid over on her butt and stretched out.

James, excited by the anticipation of pleasure, unbuttoned his pants. With a quick synchronized motion, his hands pulled down both pants and underwear in one sweep, uncovering his penis. It stood erect, ready to award him another thrill.

James walked over to Ellie, went down on his knees and lifted her dress. He spread her legs apart, leaving me in full view of her genitals.

"Christy," he said panting, "now watch this!"

James then penetrated his eight year old sister, thrusting his penis into her with hard rhythmic lunges. Breathless and flushed he continued for two or three minutes, until he exploded inside her. Gratified, he paused long enough to regain his composure.

"Christy, come over here," James said. "I dare you to touch Ellie. Come on Christy, it's fun."

Ellie continued to lay under the hay rack with her legs opened, her private parts in full view. She seemed undisturbed by my presence and a willing participant in James's game.

"Come on, Christy," James said, "Ellie's waiting. Get over here and touch her!"

Ellie turned her head at James's command and our eyes locked. She had an enticing, almost whore-like glance, even at eight years of age.

"Christy," James insisted, "if you don't come here and touch Ellie, I'll tell my dad you had sex with her in the barn. Are you going to touch her? Or are you going to force me to tell on you?"

Before I could answer, the porch door creaked open then slammed shut. The men filed out one by one and went to get their horses. Ellie jumped to her feet while James fumbled with the buttons on his pants.

"Quick, Ellie," James said, "get in the hay mow and be quiet!"

She grabbed her underwear and ran.

I was disgusted with James. I found his evil behavior revolting. I was incapable of understanding how he could engage in sexual activities with his siblings. First it was his brother Isaac then Ellie. He sickened me.

I was unable to sleep that evening. The image of James having sex with his sister kept me tossing, wide-eyed in my bed.

"James is an evil boy," I thought. "He does bad things, enjoys himself then brags about his naughty deeds. The Lord will not forgive James and he'll be condemned to hell."

I did not dare snitch on James even though I knew he had done wrong. Dad always told us that the person who witnesses an evil action and keeps it a secret is a willing accomplice and just as guilty as the person committing the sin; therefore he also is deserving of punishment. As a result, I kept James' sexual antics undisclosed, not to protect him, but to save myself from a whipping.

※ ※ ※

In the Old Order Amish Communities, the postal system was the main method of communication, since telephones were nonexistent. Letters conveyed births, Baptisms, weddings, and deaths. They brought the news, good and bad.

One day I carried the mail in to Mom and found her seated, talking to Dad.

"Davie," Mom said, "a man from Bowling Green was killed when his steam boiler at the saw mill exploded."

Her face was flushed and tear laden and she wrung her hands nervously as she spoke. It was obvious she was distraught by the information she had read in a letter addressed to the family.

"Davie, what's next?" she said. "I'm so afraid. People are imitating the 'English,' following their ways and becoming 'modern.'" Dad looked on in silence, shaking his head in disgust.

"We have been left alone," Mom continued crying. "Many of the Amish are leaving! Davie a man has died!" She was hysterical and sobbing. "Davie," she said, "I fear the Lord is sending us a message. There are too many bad things happening."

I felt a lump in my throat. I swallowed hard but it persisted. I knew it would take more than a few swallows to clear away the rising troubles. Dad tried to console Mom, but she was grief-stricken. She believed God was displeased with some of the Amish and expressing His anger. It was pointless to try to convince her otherwise.

The following Sunday, Dad was the sole Preacher at Church service. His sermon was disturbing. The fruit of his reproachful words was the devastating condemnation of Amish families. He was irritated and tired. He had to preach two sermons in three hours since there was no one else available to lighten his obligation. Dad was taut and tense, his facial muscles contracted as he stood to speak. I could see he was troubled and visibly exhausted.

"The end of the world is upon us!" Dad said, addressing the flock. "God's people have slipped and fallen by the wayside. We must pray among ourselves for the power to stay strong in order to fight and overcome temptation. Even our own have chosen to walk along an evil path. They are weak and far worse than the 'English,' who knowing only darkness and damnation are born without hope of salvation. These ex-Amish have walked in the light but have turned their backs, refusing the tradition. They have preferred to live in sin, offending and denying the Lord. They were reluctant to confess their evil deeds, unlike the Amish who slip into temptation, repent and confess, accepting their punishment as reparation for sin. These remorseful people bring me joy because they have acknowledged the Lord and returned to the light."

After concluding his lengthy sermon he sat down in his chair, bowed his head and maintained an unusual silence, while the last song was sung. It was a difficult service. It was an even more difficult day.

Easily distracted during Church service, I looked around the room and noticed the presence of some odd looking Amish people. They had long hair and moustaches and spoke a dialect of Pennsylvania Dutch with heavy German influences. Later Dad mentioned they came from across the Ocean and had sailed for almost a week to reach their destination. Among the group was a woman with her four year old son. The boy seemed to be retarded. About an hour into the service, he ran to his mother screaming:

"Mommie, Mommie I want tittie!"

I kept my eyes focused on the pair, too curious to mind my own business. It was not uncommon for women to nurse their infants in Church on Sundays; however, watching this woman uncover her breast while her four year old son stood beside her sucking milk was shocking. It was a scene I would never forget.

It was a frequent occurrence to witness one year old babies brutally slapped in Church for restless behavior. They were deemed responsible for their actions. Their little red tear-stained faces and piercing shrieks were sadly a common Sunday event.

I was becoming more unsettled, confused and bothered by the turn of events in the community. There were so many unanswered questions and unexplained feelings to deal with.

I was always curious and eager for different experiences. I felt restless and my burgeoning hormones began to come into play. The unpredictable stirrings in my groin were frustrating and made me edgy. I didn't know why I had these feelings or how to handle the sudden urges. One day, feeling a bit anxious I remembered the day James had sex with the bottle calf. I pictured his animated face and recalled his words telling me how much fun it was and how good it made him feel. The unknown was enticing. I thought maybe I could appease my inner rumblings and feel good also.

That evening after chores, I hurried into the barn, grabbed some twine and shoved it into my pocket. I walked over to the bottle pen, approached a calf and coaxed her out. Quickly I reached into my pocket, withdrew the twine and pulled the calf close to me. She bucked nervously a couple of times but I was fast and avoided her kicks. When she settled down, I wound the twine around her hind legs several times and unbuttoned my pants. I yanked down my underwear and felt a cool breeze on my naked skin.

I pulled the calf toward me and thrust my erect penis into her. Her body twitched and went rigid. I remember James had lunged forward and I imitated his behavior shoving my penis until I felt a burst of pleasure. Satisfied, I moved away from the calf. Picking up my pants, I fastened the buttons, untied the calf and led her back to the bottle pen.

I didn't expect the awful reaction that followed. Feeling dirty, I dashed over to the water tank, lowered my pants and underwear again and splashed myself with the refreshing liquid. Desperately, I tried to cleanse away the traces of the filthy sin I had just committed. I knew I had done a really bad thing. I was disgusted and could not understand how James could enjoy such a vile pastime.

That evening I was restless and anxious. After supper as usual Dad settled in his chair reading the Bible. I sat swinging my legs and rocking back and forth, alternating my movements. Dad paused his reading and looked up.

"Christy," he said, "you're awfully fidgety this evening. Is something wrong?"

"No, Dad," I said, too ashamed and scared to admit what I had done. "Nothing's wrong. I think I'll go up to bed."

"OK, Christy," Dad said. "Goodnight and don't forget to say your prayers."

I felt even more terrible. How could I recite the "Our Father" after the awful sin I had committed today.

I went upstairs, undressed and climbed into bed. William's breathing was steady and deep. I knew he was already asleep and I was careful not to disturb him. I did not expect to shut my eyes, knowing I would watch darkness burst into light. I did not fight the tears.

On his way to bed, Dad heard my muffled sobs and came into the room.

"Christy, what's wrong?" he said. "Did you do something bad today?"

"No, Dad," I said. Satisfied with my lie he left.

I continued to relive my dirty act with the calf. It would not leave my mind. The torment was incessant; the nausea unrelenting.

"I am a sinner and the Lord will punish me," I said to myself. Although I was afraid to address the Lord I whispered:

"Forgive us our trespasses as we forgive those who trespass against us and lead us not into temptation but deliver us from evil."

I hoped the Lord was listening. I vowed I would never again engage in such a dirty and evil deed, if God would forgive me this time. I was truly sorry for my grave sin.

However, remorse is short lived for an eleven year old.

❋   ❋   ❋

The summer of 1983 was our last in Maywood. I did not see much of Isaac and James. Uncle Ralph had caught them having sex with the animals and they had been grounded. I had to find different ways to amuse myself.

I remember Maywood as a joyful period of my life. It was a time of new adventures and different experiences. Dad and I had built a stronger relationship and I had come to respect and honor him as a Bishop and as a father. I looked up to him. He was my hero and he was a cool Dad. However, when he announced we were leaving Maywood, I was saddened and distraught. At that time I did not yet know my feelings were justified.

Dad was disenchanted with Maywood. He was bothered by the appalling changes in the community. Amish people were following the 'English' man's ways, sinning, denying the Lord, and refusing the Tradition. They seemed so undisturbed by the idea they were going to hell. Fear of the Lord was gone. Only four families remained. Amish from other communities came to visit, after learning that many Maywood Amish had fallen into 'modern' ways. Dad was distressed and thought it best to load the van with the family and possessions and head for a new community, a new beginning and a different life away from the evil ex Amish. He had no idea where his decision to flee evil would eventually take him: And more importantly he did not know where it would lead me.

On moving day, I slipped away unnoticed and ran back to the timber. With a saddened heart I sat for the last time, under a huge old oak and listened to the gurgling creek. I noticed the rumblings seemed louder. I was hurting and I was angry. Someone was to blame for my misery: Dad.

We were heading to Kahoka, a community fifty miles from Maywood. That was quite a distance to travel with horse and buggy and I knew I would never see my beloved Maywood again. I would meet new people and see different surroundings.

The confusion weighed heavy in my heart. Moving away from Maywood did not make sense. As a young boy I was expected to obey and not question my elders. However, if Dad would have taken the time to explain the reasons for his choices, perhaps

I would have been more accepting and certainly less tormented. Dad's decisions, good or bad, were rules I had to obey.

I left the timber, walked over to the van and stepped inside. I turned my head for a final glance as we drove away. I had to build a memory I hoped I would never forget.

The van moved along the driveway, crunching gravel as it did the day we arrived. It proceeded at a steady pace along the road. Suddenly I was pushed forward in my seat. The van descended the hill. My spirits dropped. My hopes, wishes and dreams were gone. I turned to snatch one more look at the farm house, but it too had disappeared.

I looked at Dad with hate in my heart. He was a leader and a powerful person. But he was unable to stop the Amish in his community from following 'modern' man into damnation. He lost his flock; God's chosen had deserted him! Now he wanted to move forward. Although I did not know at the time, this was the start of a very different journey: It was the end of a new beginning but more importantly it was the new beginning of a very different end.

❋   ❋   ❋

III

Kahoka, Missouri

Fall of 1983–
Fall of 1993

Chapter 10

A new and very different period of my life was about to begin and I faced it with curiosity, anger, resentment and an almost crippling confusion. I was growing up and there were so many questions to answer and so many puzzling feelings to understand. Life was changing and I was facing another move to a different community. There were countless sad goodbyes and I knew I would not see many of my Maywood companions again.

The trip from Maywood to Kahoka was long and exhausting. The van was in endless motion and it seemed as if we would never reach our destination. When we finally pulled into the driveway, I felt a return of excitement. The van continued along the gravel lane and stopped in front of the house.

"Christy," William said pointing to the barn. "Look, there are electrical wires running through the barn! Did Dad buy a 'modern' house?"

"I don't know, William," I said.

This house looked different from our houses in Bowling Green and Maywood. It was recently constructed and did not have a run-down façade which is characteristic of Old Order Amish houses.

I bolted from the van eager to explore my new surroundings. A strong gust of wind snatched my hat. I continued to run, bareheaded towards the house.

"Christy," Mom said, bending over to retrieve the hat. "Come back here and get your hat."

I stopped, turned and ran back to Mom. She dusted the brim with several sweeps of her hand. It felt good to have the frisky wind ruffle my hair.

"The 'English' are always bareheaded," I thought. "It would be nice not to have to wear a hat all the time." However, I questioned if it was worth going to hell for such a small pleasure! I took the hat from Mom and set it back on my head.

The tractor trailer was unloaded and our furniture, beddings and other possessions were carried inside and unpacked. I was amazed to see how relatively new the house was and how 'modern' it looked. There was a walk out basement which was always exciting. I noticed the flooring on the upper level had not yet been installed. The house seemed to be pretty nice and certainly newer than the previous ones. The electrical wires, however, shocked me. I wondered if Dad would permit the use of electricity.

"Christy, William!" Dad said, interrupting my thought, "Don't touch any of the switches!"

"OK, Dad," I said. William nodded in agreement.

That evening, I lay in bed beside William. We chatted about the day's events, discussing and comparing our Maywood and Bowling Green houses with this new one. Afterwards, I tossed and turned, too excited to shut my eyes. I kept staring at the light bulb on the ceiling. I wondered what made it glow so brightly. In my imagination I tried to picture the bulb lit up.

"William," I said, "I dare you to flick the light switch!"

"Christy, I dare you to turn it on," he said without removing his eyes from the bulb.

He played right into my hands. I knew he would be intimidated by Dad's order not to touch anything.

I jumped out of bed. In the darkness, I ran over to the switch, and flipped it on. The room burst into illumination. It was dazzling. Quickly I flipped it off, then on again. It was magical and I was thrilled to be able to control the light with a flick of my finger.

Suddenly Dad walked in:

"Who turned the light on?" he said.

"I didn't do it, Dad, Christy did: He flipped the switch!" William said without pausing to breathe.

"Christy," Dad said, "didn't I tell you to stay away from those switches?"

"Yes, Dad" I said, beginning to cry.

"Why did you switch the light on Christy?" he said. Get up and come over here, right now!"

He grabbed me by the shoulder and pulled me close. I stood holding my breath, anticipating the pain. With his left hand he yanked my ear and quickly delivered two swift slaps to my face. In the quiet of night, the impact of his palm on my skin echoed.

"Christy," Dad said, withdrawing his calloused hand from my face, "did you learn your lesson?"

"Yes, Dad," I lied.

My cheeks stung and I was forced to sleep on my back until the stinging subsided.

❋ ❋ ❋

An 'English' man, Jeff Murray, lived about a mile across the field, just to the north of our house. Since my room faced his house, I often stood near the window and observed through the lenses of Dad's binoculars, 'modern' man's way of life. I watched him enter and depart his vehicles and operate his motorized farm equipment. He was a kind, pleasant man who one day presented himself at our door with a puppy. The dog was a collie with a mass of fluffy golden fur that tickled the palm of my hand whenever I ran it over his back and head. It was love at first sight. I named him Buster and soon he became my best friend.

It was 1984. I was twelve years old and beginning to feel uncomfortable with my surroundings. Although I was unable to define the source of my anxiety, I felt something was not quite right. I had problems communicating and expressing my true feelings and the uncertainties tormenting my spirit were mounting. I did not understand Dad's way of thinking and behaving.

Often he seemed so inconsistent and contradictory. I wanted to know why he did what he did and upon what criteria he based his decisions.

As the days passed and life continued, I no longer lived in harmony with my family. I started to withdraw from Dad. I was troubled but still incapable of deciphering the cause of my frustration. I knew I could not discuss my thoughts and feelings with anyone and having no one to turn to left me lonely.

I turned to Buster, feeling free to unburden my soul. He was a perfect listener who never yelled or chastised me. Buster never got angry or snarled and he never whipped or slapped me for "breaking the rules." Above all he never lied to me! One afternoon, while walking Buster in the timber I confided my disturbing thoughts.

"Buster, Dad's cruel," I said. "He lives like a god, doing whatever he pleases. No one has the power to stop him. He is the Bishop and his word is the law. Everyone fears his rule. This is nonsense."

We sat beside the creek and listened to the gurgling water. Buster seemed to understand my pain. He was quiet and nuzzled me from time to time. His moist nose resting in the crevice of my arm left a circular stain on my shirt sleeve.

"Buster, I am not like these people," I said. "I don't think like them and I don't want to live like them. Dad makes all the rules and if I break them he beats me. It's humiliating and it hurts."

Buster looked up at me with his big brown eyes. He made several soft sounds encouraging me to continue. Accepting his "invitation" I spoke my mind freely and without fear of reprisal.

"Buster this is ridiculous," I said. "I will not listen to Dad when I get older. For the moment I will try to do my best not to anger him or get caught. But he's cruel, Buster, even if he is the Bishop! It's all just a bunch of bull shit."

Buster jumped on my lap and licked my nose and face. With his little tongue moving up and down my cheeks, he wiped away my tears. He understood what no one else did and more importantly he was sympathetic to my pain when no one seemed to care. He accepted me knowing I was different and he believed my torments were real.

※　※　※

My uncle, Andrew Burkholder, helped Dad lay flooring in our new home. Uncle Andrew was a short tempered, outgoing man with dark hair and eyes. He was a large man who stood six feet tall and weighed about two hundred pounds. His presence was noticeable and somewhat intimidating.

Uncle Andrew and his family had also arrived in Kahoka from Bowling Green, fleeing the evil that had run rampant in the community. His move was so hurried he did not have a house to accommodate the family. Offering to help, Dad approached the 'English' man who had sold him our property. The man owned an old school bus he parked over the hill, towards the timber. Dad asked him if Uncle Andrew and his five children could live in the school bus until he had a suitable house. Permission granted, Uncle Andrew and his family set up home in the bus, draping curtains over the windows for privacy and stringing twine between two trees to make a clothes line. This was their home, until Uncle Andrew purchased a piece of property from Dad and built the family house. Living in a bus was not a customary practice in the Old Order Amish Tradition and Uncle Andrew in a sense had been a pioneer.

I was unhappy and needed answers to the many whys beginning to overpower me: Why are the Amish so malicious and vindictive? Dad always preached:

"For if you forgive men their offenses, your heavenly Father will also forgive you your offenses…But if you do not forgive men, neither will your Father forgive you."

If the Amish are such God fearing people why are they so unforgiving? Why are they so self-centered and so unconcerned about the feelings and well-being of others? Why do they preach the truth then turn around and live lies?

Despite my confusion and serious doubts, at twelve years of

age, I was already certain I could no longer accept the Amish tradition. The hypocrisy, the violence and the inconsistencies disgusted me. There were so many changes which made so little sense.

My mind wandered: I wondered why the stocking caps we wore in Maywood during the winter time were no longer permitted in Kahoka and I questioned why Dad had sold all the chain saws we used before our move.

"Dad," I said, curious for answers, "why don't we have chain saws here in Kahoka?"

"Christy," he replied, "we did not have chain saws in Bowling Green. I allowed them in Maywood but believe I made a terrible mistake."

"Why was it a mistake, Dad?" I asked, trying to understand a decision I did not agree with.

"Remember, evil begins with the smallest thing," he said. "It doesn't take much to fall into sin. This is why I decided to go back to the circular blade. It works just as well as the chains. In Maywood, many of our good Amish people have followed the 'modern' man into damnation. I cannot have that happen again. Do you understand, Christy?"

"Yes, Dad," I lied. "But why can't we wear stocking caps?"

"Christy," Dad said, irritated by my barrage of questions, "if it gets very cold you can ask Mom for an old sock, cut it in half and wear it over your ears. It'll keep you just as warm as the stocking cap. Now enough of this nonsense, I've chores to finish."

I turned around and walked back to the house, even more confused.

"If both the stocking cap and cut sock keep me warm," I thought, "then what difference does it make which one I wear? Why is it forbidden to wear a cap but not a cut stocking?"

I vowed to find my own answers one day.

From a seed planted in Bowling Green and fertilized in Maywood, a stem was beginning to sprout!

❋   ❋   ❋

Chapter 11

I was maturing and, as a young teen, my thinking was in conflict with the sermons Dad and the Preachers delivered in Church on Sundays. Although an education to stimulate free thinking was unheard of, my mind worked around the limits imposed, to achieve its own potential.

The Elders did not intend school to offer much nourishment for serious thought. Therefore, the eight year program of study did not reflect standard elementary and middle school education. Ignorance and a dreaded fear of the Lord kept the Amish loyal to the Tradition and settled in the community.

We studied the alphabet, some elementary math and learned to read and write English and German. Geography lessons were taught using two approaches. The first involved spinning the globe, pointing to a state in the USA and being asked to identify its capital while the second involved a series of cards, each with a state written on it. These cards were then flashed in front of us and we were required to name the capital city. History seemed to center on William Penn. Classes were twenty minutes for each subject. The rest of the day was spent coloring and drawing with a half hour break for lunch and recess. At fourteen, formal education was completed. Afterwards girls worked in the home with their mothers and boys either farmed with their dads or were assumed as an apprentice and taught a trade.

On the Sunday mornings when Church services were not held it was customary to finish chores, have breakfast and recite some prayers. Afterwards we proceeded to the living room to listen to Dad read passages from the Bible.

One Sunday, William and I sat quietly beside Dad while he read from the Bible. His expression was somber and he paused as he came to a passage he felt was important to emphasize. I remember he stopped reading, drifted into a quick reflection then lifted his head slightly from the printed page.

"Christy, William," Dad said, "did you understand what I just read? This passage explains why we keep the Amish tradition. You know the 'English' do not obey the rules. They are sinners who deliberately refuse to fear the Lord. They are not God's children."

Dad continued to explain and compare the differences between the Amish Tradition and the evil ways of 'modern' man.

"This is why," he said, "the Amish are saved when they pass on while the 'English' are condemned to hell!"

I was happy when Dad finished reading and closed the Bible. I did not quite comprehend the significance of his words or what he tried to teach us. It was all still a mystery. Today, I just wanted to head for the stalls, get my horse and go riding.

"Christy," Dad said, "you can go ride now; but remember I don't want you going far. Is that clear?"

"Yes, Dad," I lied.

We mounted our horses, met up with cousins Paul and Will and rode off in search of fun and adventure. Although we were given strict orders not to leave the property, we galloped the horses down through the timber, unknown to Dad. Along the way we came to a fence. I dismounted and pulled open a tiny gap, creating a space wide enough to pass through. After a two mile ride, we reached an old gravel road. The echoing clip-clop of the horses' galloping hooves crunching the stones disturbed the Sunday afternoon silence. I loved racing and I enjoyed riding bareback. It was a lot of fun and it was exhilarating to feel the rush of wind on my face.

We rode down the gravel road for quite awhile until we came to the dumpsite.

"William, Will, Paul," I said, jumping down from my horse, "let's see if there's anything good in the trash pile today."

"OK, Christy," they said.

"Christy," William said, "if I find something good can I keep it?"

"Yeah, sure you can. Just don't let anyone see it or we'll get a whipping from Dad."

We rummaged through the trash, ransacking the contents, searching for something cool to take. Lifting a small tin box I uncovered a picture of a nude woman. I was amazed and couldn't remove my eyes from the glossy print.

"Look what I found," I shouted.

William, Will and Paul ran over and scrambled up to the trash pile where I stood waving the picture.

"Look at this woman. She's totally naked! Look, she has no hair!" I said, surprised. My eyes were wide and my quick short breaths betrayed my excitement.

"Look at her legs. They're so smooth!" I said flashing the picture in their faces. "She has no hair except down there on her crotch!"

"This is weird," Paul said. "The woman doesn't have any hair! What happened to her hair?"

I glanced at the picture:

"I heard 'English' women shave," I said. "They don't walk around with hair all over. That's why she has no hair! Wow, she sure looks good!"

We stood in a circle staring at the picture, astonished over how great the hairless woman looked.

One evening before supper William tugged on my shirt sleeve.

"Christy, do you still have the picture of the naked lady without any hair?"

"No, William," I lied, "I left it in the trash pile."

Actually, I had quickly stuffed it in my pocket.

After supper I walked out to the barn. Coming across a splinter of wood, I picked it up and jabbed it through the top of the picture.

"This will keep it upright," I thought to myself.

The naked woman came alive in front of me. The evening light was perfect and accentuated her sleek body. She looked even more enticing in the dim glow.

The more I stared at the woman, the more intense the stirrings in my groin became. Quickly I unhooked my suspenders, unbuttoned my pants and dropped them to my ankles along with my underwear. After satisfying myself, I hurriedly hid the picture.

For a moment thoughts of James and his naughty antics crossed my mind. I wondered what he was up to. I had not seen him or Isaac since I left Maywood.

Although I never agreed with James' bad behavior, with the passing years, my hormones surged, escalating my sexual desires. To release the increasing frustration I continued this practice of self-gratification. Masturbating calmed my sexual tension, gave me pleasure and was more exciting than having sex with a bottle calf. I found it neither disturbed me nor left me feeling disgusted and dirty.

It was 1987. I was fifteen and in full puberty. The hormonal surges were neither simple to understand nor easy to deal with. My mind was expanding, speeding away from the Amish Tradition and proceeding in a very different direction. I was growing and both my body and mind were changing.

I will never forget the day we received the shocking news about Grandpa Kemp's passing. Although I was almost a grown man, I ran off to the barn, buried my head in my arms and cried. Grandpa had not visited often in Kahoka but was present when we first moved from Maywood. He had helped load the van and unpack our belongings upon our arrival. I had happy and pleasant memories of him. Unlike Grandpa Burkholder, Grandpa Kemp never treated us cruelly and never berated any of our childish failings.

Mom was disheartened and sad over his passing even though Grandpa had been suffering from cancer. The morning of the funeral, the 'English' man arrived with his van to drive the family to Bowling Green for the service. It was an emotionally draining journey that stirred up many buried feelings. Returning to the community where I spent my childhood brought to mind countless memories, some of which were agonizing to relive. The beatings, the lies, the pain and humiliation flashed in front of my face. I felt nauseated but took a deep breath and prepared for Grandpa's funeral.

The Amish would never consider purchasing a coffin; therefore Grandpa was laid to rest in a handmade oak casket. The lid was set firmly in place. I sat with my gaze lowered trying to avoid any eye contact with the casket. My attention wandered during the service and I paid little heed to the sermon being delivered on Grandpa's behalf. At funerals, there were no readings from the Bible. Instead the Preacher eulogized about the deceased and his salvation, praising the spiritual benefits of leading a virtuous life according to the Amish Tradition. Grandpa was held up as an example of a worthy man who had died in good favor with the Lord thus earning a glorious reward of eternal life.

There was silence except for a few shuffling feet, until the Preacher cleared his throat.

"We join together today feeling happy and blessed," he said, elevating his voice. "We rejoice because an Amish man is now with the Lord. Grandpa Kemp has been freed from his earthly suffering. The cancer that destroyed his body no longer exists. His pain and agony have ended: Instead, he is blessed to move forward to his new home in heaven."

During funeral services, we were always reminded how fortunate we were to be born Amish.

The Preacher continued his praise of Amish Tradition, stressing the merits of living the plain and simple life.

"How fortunate we are to be able to face death, as children of the Lord, never betraying our tradition. We cherish this moment. Today, we realize a wonderful truth; one of our own has gained salvation. He now sits with the Lord in heaven enjoying the splendor of his reward. He begins a new life. There will be neither salvation nor an after life in the grace of the Lord for the 'English.' Only the fires of hell will greet them when they pass on!"

The funeral service lasted three hours. After the sermons were delivered and prayers said, it was concluded. No song books were passed around like on Sundays and there was no singing.

I watched as the Preachers and the Bishop tearfully concluded their sermons. I lowered my head during the prayers setting free my own tears.

"Grandpa suffered from a horrible cancer," I thought to myself.

I was happy his agony had come to an end.

"Death has to be wonderful," I thought to myself. I imagined a life without punishment, humiliation, confusion and pain! No rules, no beatings! What freedom! I was joyful Grandpa made it to heaven!

After the service, two unrelated Elders rose from their seats, walked over to the casket, and lifted the lid to uncover the body for the viewing. I observed in silence as Mom and the girls slowly paraded around Grandpa's coffin. Their heads were bowed until they came into direct view of Grandpa's body. Their tear-stained faces were taut as, one by one, they gazed at him for the last time.

Mom was heartbroken. Grandpa was her dad, a kind and gentle man. My gloom was painful, my despondency, overpowering. Although it was not customary for a teen age boy to weep outwardly, I lost all intent and strength to control my emotions. I didn't care if anyone saw me and had no fear about someone mocking me for my behavior. I broke down and sobbed uncontrollably.

The silence was broken by the echo of steel-rimmed wheels crunching the gravel as the buggies departed for the cemetery

I had to deal with Grandpa's death, difficult as it was, but the beautiful memories he gave me were a solace and respite from my pain: Knowing he was blessed to be with the Lord was an inspiring thought. I felt comforted in my misery.

Standard Bred horse hitched to a top buggy

Amish husband and wife preparing to travel

My courting buggy I built at age eighteen

Amish school books

Amish family walking to Church

New Amish homestead

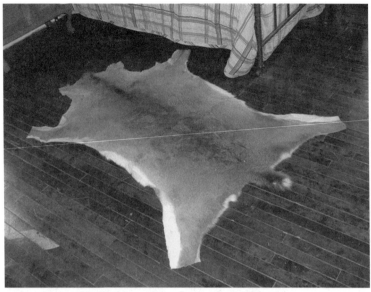
Deer skin on the floor of my old room

Amish living room

Chris Burkholder

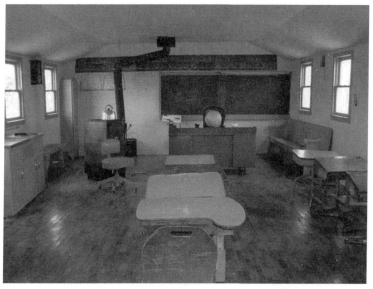

Amish one room schoolhouse from which
I graduated from in 1987 at age 14

Leather whipping strap on student school desk

Amish children walking to Church

Traditional Amish straw and black felt hats

Amish bedroom I grew up in

Amish home I grew up in and escaped from

Chapter 12

At sixteen years of age my doubts intensified and my questions multiplied, remaining unanswered. I was disillusioned with my way of life; a life I was no longer willing to live. I was upset with Dad for returning to a Bowling Green lifestyle in which his inconsistencies and double standard decision making irritated me. I knew I could no longer accept his rules and give him the obedience he wanted. Instead, I became insubordinate, resorting back to aggression and hostility as a means of vindicating the abuse I was forced to endure. My independent thinking led me to establish my own self-rule, pushing me one step closer to autonomy and two steps away from Dad and the Amish Tradition, filled with too many taboos.

On New Year's Day the Amish reunited to celebrate the holiday and greet the New Year. It was customary for the men to go rabbit hunting on this special occasion.

The day marking the beginning of 1989 was no exception. Will Burkholder was Uncle Andrew's son. He was a bushy haired, reckless boy with a jovial personality who like me loved different adventures. One day, Will, Paul, William and I plus two other boys drove Uncle Andrew's open buggy down to the timber to hunt rabbits. After killing several we soon tired of this activity, jumped on the buggy and rode off. Along the road we noticed an interesting antique car, parked along the timber line. We quickly jumped off the buggy and gathered around the car to get a closer look. The body of the auto was dent free and it was evident the car had been scrupulously maintained, even though the car had not been driven for quite some time.

"William," I said, moving close to the car, "let's play western!"

"No, Christy," he said. "I don't think so." He paused a moment and then continued. "Well, what do you mean, play Western?"

"Well," I said, "we have the shotguns with us today. Let's get in the buggy, race by and shoot at the car. We can pretend there are bad guys riding inside."

"OK, Christy," William said. "That sounds pretty exciting to me. Let's do it!"

Before leaving for the rabbit hunt, we had removed the back seat of the buggy, creating a truck like bed in the rear. The other four boys stood in the back aiming their guns. The horse raced past the car and we opened fire, each of us emptying three rounds of ammunition into the car. The noise of the bullets leaving the gun and smashing through the windows was ear piercing. The windows shattered sending pieces of glass flying through the air.

"We got you now, you son of a bitch!" I yelled. Catching my enthusiasm, the other boys joined in.

"We're outlaws! Do you understand! We're not going to put up with you trespassing on our property, "we shouted, continuing to reload and fire our shotguns.

Since neither our parents nor the Elders were present, we cursed and swore at the "imaginary enemies."

The car was pretty much destroyed with all its windows in pieces and its body full of dark bullet holes. We took one final ride around, laughing and cheering our naughty rampage, before heading for the house.

I remember the snow had fallen ahead of schedule that year. The corn had grown tall and needed to be shucked even though the snow was knee deep and the temperatures were freezing.

Mom, Dad, Rebecca, Elma and I went out to shuck corn. Dad and I each handled two rows at a time, switching back and forth from side to side. The women shucked one row each, filling the wagon as quickly as possible.

"Dad," I said pausing a moment to get the blood circulating in my numb hands, "why can't we use a tractor and drive though the field with the corn picker? That would be a lot easier and we wouldn't freeze to death!"

"I'm warning you, Christy," Dad said irritated, "I'll not have that kind of talk. Do you hear me?"

Happy to have an invitation to express my thoughts, I said, "this is stupid. It's freezing outside and we're all standing knee deep in snow. We had plenty of time before the onset of winter to shuck the corn and nobody did it."

"That's right, Christy," Dad said. "And you didn't do it either; so now we have to do it in the freezing cold."

When the day's shucking was finished the wagon was unloaded in the corn crib. After supper we all rose from the table. William and I no longer spent time in the living room but returned to our room to read the John Wayne books which in addition to the cool swear words, taught us how to stand up for our beliefs and ideas. Dad turned to face me.

"Christy," he said, "I want you to remain down here in the living room. William, you can go upstairs." I knew I was in trouble.

"Christy," Dad said, "what's the matter? I don't like this talk about tractors."

I said, "This does not make any sense to me. The Bible does not forbid the use of tractors. It does not say you cannot have a tractor or you cannot have rubber tires."

Dad fixed his gaze on me. It was icy and sent a chill down my back.

"Christy," he said, "the Bible doesn't say you can't smoke marijuana either."

I looked at Dad and chuckled openly.

"Dad," I said still chuckling, "the Bible says, "Thou shalt not kill!"

"What do you mean by that, Christy?" he responded.

I repeated, "I guess the Bible does say you cannot kill somebody."

"Christy," Dad said, his brow furrowed in a puzzled expression, "there is a problem here. Somewhere along the way we missed something. We beat you, we punished you, we did everything possible to make you respect and obey the rules. Now tell me, Christy, what is your problem? I want to know what's wrong!"

"Nothing, Dad," I lied, knowing that if I told him what was really disturbing me I'd get a nasty whipping. He wouldn't understand anyway. I kept silent about how his cruelty and brutality bothered and humiliated me. I did not mention how disturbing his self-centered manner and lack of concern for others was. I did not tell him he was thoughtless and as a Bishop with authority this was inexcusable. I did not understand how he could pronounce his own people 'dead' and shun them. That was taking life and ending it. I could not reveal that the young folks whom he felt were good Amish people were defying his rules. They were smoking cigarettes and drinking alcohol to the limits of intoxication. He led these young folks and preached to them during Sunday service and was proud of who they were. I wondered if he was incapable of seeing the truth or just plain unwilling to come to terms with reality. I questioned if it was blindness or denial.

"Is Dad stupid?" I thought. My doubts planted in Bowling Green were sprouting and spreading. Despite my qualms I knew for sure that I did not want to emulate these Amish people.

Winter had passed and finally the warm days of summer arrived. It was time to haul manure. I worked barefoot and rolled up my pants to avoid getting the stinky manure all over the bottoms. As I loaded it on to the manure spreader my toes squished in the soft mounds. Sometimes it was supple and slippery, other times it was dry and less pliable. Regardless of the texture, it always had a putrid odor.

William and I had argued earlier about unloading the manure. Even though we took turns unloading, he claimed he did two loads more than I. Once the lever was popped, the wheel drawn manure spreader would feed it off through the beaters and scatter it about. It was not a difficult chore. However, that day the wind blew in the wrong direction and the manure flew back, splattering all over our hats and shirts. It was certainly not a pleasant experience.

That evening, while milking, William and I continued to argue over the day's manure unloading chore. He muttered under his breath and continued to complain about his extra two loads.

I said, "Are you still sore about that? Why don't you just shut up and forget about it. You're younger than me and have to take it."

He turned on his milking stool and aimed the cow's tit in my direction, spraying me with a full shot of milk. Since I was seated on a short milking stool, the surge of warm liquid hit me right in the crotch, drenching me. My temper flared. I rose from my stool, lifted my bucket, leaned over the side of the cow and dumped about a gallon and a half of milk over the top of his head.

Even though Dad was not present to witness my daring action, he walked into the barn a few minutes later and understood what had happened.

"What's going on here?" he said, raising his voice.

My heart raced. I knew I was in big trouble.

"Dad," William said, "Christy made me unload a couple of loads of manure more than he did today and now he's rubbing it in!"

"I want to know who dumped the milk," Dad said.

"Christy did," William said, "Christy dumped the milk on me."

"Well I can see that with my own eyes," Dad said grabbing one of the remaining chain hobbles that hung on the back wall. "Christy, get over here now!"

Angrily, Dad grabbed the chain hobbles which came equipped with a steel cup on each end. When it was swung around it hooked on the cow's legs just above the knees. On one end there was a slot where the chain slid and could be tightened to bind the hind legs together while milking. This prevented the cow from kicking and spilling the milk.

With the chain hobbles in his hand, Dad slid the heavy metal cups to one end, clearing a two foot piece of chain. He had a wild look in his eyes and his anger was evident. I knew he was irritated with me and I knew I'd get a brutal lashing.

"Christy, stand up along this wall," he said fixing his gaze in the direction in which he wanted me to go. I did as I was told.

"I have had enough of your nonsense, Christy," he said. "Maybe this will straighten you out."

Dad's tone was serious and his voice emphatic. I noticed he spoke much louder than usual. He lifted his arm and swung the chain around my back. I squirmed and grimaced in pain but did not cry. My approach to Dad's brutality was different this time. I held my breath and forced myself to maintain a rigid position. As he swung his arm, the chain wrapped around and slammed across the side of my belly. At the end of the chain there was a ring to keep it from sliding through the slot of the hobble. The weight of the ring hitting my body intensified the pain. I received five lashing before he lowered the chain.

"Did you have enough, Christy?" he said, still gripping the chain. "Or do you want me to give you some more?"

He lifted the chain hobbles as he spoke, threatening me with another round of torture.

I did not look at him and I did not give him the satisfaction of listening to my sobs. Instead I kept a stiff upper lip and stood tall.

I nodded my head, boldly refusing to give him the courtesy of a response. He walked to the back of the barn and hung up the chain hobbles.

Dad was not worthy of my breath. I despised him and hated the hypocrisy he soaked in.

"William," I said, "we work hard milking and doing chores yet Dad just loafs around. I hate the son of a bitch! It seems as if his main purpose in life is to deliver cruel punishments."

"Christy," William said, "I'm going to tell Dad if you don't shut up!"

"William, I had enough. If you don't shut up I'm going to beat you with my chair! Do you hear me?"

William looked at me with an odd expression. "Oh yeah, Christy?" he said.

"Don't provoke me, William," I responded. "Just try me and you'll see what happens."

He quieted down. I would have willingly endured the anguish of another lashing from Dad if that's what it took to set William straight.

I returned to milking the cow, unable to concentrate. I gazed over at William and came to the shocking realization that I had threatened to beat him for answering me in a manner I did not appreciate: I was not any better than Dad! In truth I was just like him, using violence to resolve a situation.

Dad's way irritated me more and more each day. I was disgusted with him and with my own cruel behavior.

❋ ❋ ❋

One day, Dad asked me to help him clean some lumber he acquired to build an extra horse shed. To clean lumber we hammered the nails upright then yanked them out.

"Christy," Dad said, resting the hammer down, "what's stuck in your teeth?"

"Nothing," I said, continuing to pull nails.

"What do you mean nothing?" Dad said, "Don't lie to me Christy. Come over here and we'll see what's going on."

He reached out and pulled me closer. Grabbing me by the chin, he tilted my head back. With his grimy hand he grabbed my lower lip and yanked it down forcefully, exposing the chew hidden along my gum.

"Where did you get that? I want to know who gave you the chew."

"Nobody, Dad," I said, "I found it beside the road."

"You know that chewing is prohibited, Christy, don't you?" Dad said. "Spit it out right now!" I obeyed.

"Come here inside the lumber shed," Dad said.

I walked over to where the clean lumber was stored, anticipating my punishment. Dad grabbed a three foot stick and thrashed my lower back. The sound of the board swatting my butt had little effect on me. I neither cried nor showed any remorse, but spent my thoughts concentrating on getting another dip of chew.

"Don't ever do that again, Christy," Dad said putting the stick back in its place. "That's the 'English' man's way. It's a bad habit to follow. It's a sin and will only get you out of favor with the Lord. You will be a slave to the chew instead of the Lord!"

❋   ❋   ❋

Chapter 13

I crossed over many thorny paths on my journey to becoming a free thinker. My withdrawal from Dad was serious and led to acts of defiance and rebellion. I was disillusioned with the powerful Bishop and the return of his duplicitous way of thinking and acting disgusted me. I was the Bishop's son and my ruthless behavior and reliance on violence to satisfy my quest for revenge was a stepping stone to his eventual downfall in the community. He was losing power over his son and his own flock began to question his authority. However, I had to restore the dignity he snatched from me through years of cruel and humiliating abuse and I had to avenge the wrongs committed against me. The physical wounds were painful especially for a young child, but the emotional sores were even more agonizing. I was seventeen years old and already knew the end was in sight.

Dad and I had been at odds with each other. The tension between us intensified as the day's scorching temperatures made us less tolerant. We were digging a trench to the hog house to install a water hydrant and our sweat soaked shirts hung heavy on our shoulders. The beads of perspiration rolled down, saturating our pants. They clung to our legs, irritating our skin as we moved. It was mid-week and we had not bathed since Saturday. The odor of sweat was pungent and trailed us as we went about doing chores.

I was upset and furious and could not understand why Dad did not engage the 'English' man to dig this one hundred by four foot line with a trencher. I was confused and questioned why we could not use the 'English' man for this chore when we did so in many other instances. However, Dad would not hear of it, preferring to do it manually. I should have known better. The Bishop was stubborn and everything had to be done his way.

We worked together until Dad left to tend to other chores. I remained under the torrid sun, continuing to dig the trench.

In the Old Order Amish Tradition, men's shirts were designed with three buttons. On hot days, it was permissible to open the top one. However, unbuttoning the second and exposing a hairy chest was considered a defiant and bold action in a community where nothing less than full compliance and a modest mindset predominated.

I continued digging and sweating. My back itched from the coarse wet material rubbing against my skin.

"Screw this shit," I said, dropping my shovel. "I'm going to open another button and if Dad doesn't approve that's just too bad. If he whips me I can take it. I've been lashed before and I'll be lashed again. Who cares: One more or one less won't make a difference."

I unbuttoned my shirt and went back to digging. Dad returned, gazed into the trench to see how deep I had dug, picked up his shovel and went to work.

"Christy, why is your shirt open that way?" Dad said. "You know that's not acceptable. We're not 'English', Christy, we're Amish and we dress according to tradition."

"It's hot," I said leaning on my shovel. Dad stopped digging.

"What?" he said, "Are you telling me you're disobeying the rules because it's hot?"

I understood from Dad's irritated tone I better not continue my defiant behavior. It was obvious there was no way I could win this battle.

Focusing my eyes on the trench, I buttoned my shirt believing silence and obedience were the best ways to settle the issue.

Dad was not convinced. He wanted conversation and made several attempts to engage me in a discussion. I remained quiet, too busy with my own thoughts to waste time on his nonsense.

"What's the matter?" Dad said. "I'm trying to understand here. Why can't you be like the rest of the boys? They are well-behaved and obey the rules without all this opposition I get from you."

I thought to myself, "Yeah right, if you only knew what we all did last Sunday night!"

My silence continued. Dad took a deep breath.

He said, "You're seventeen years old and almost old enough to be baptized. You need to think about becoming a member of Church. You do realize it's almost time, don't you?"

"Yeah, Dad," I said breaking my silence, "I guess I'll be old enough next year."

"What do you mean, Christy?" Dad said irritated, "Don't you want to be baptized?"

"I don't know," I said. "actually, I never thought about it."

"Well, Christy," Dad said, "it's time you gave it some serious thought. It's time to stop this childish nonsense. You need to grow up and become somebody."

He cleared his throat and lightened his tone.

He said, "You know that after Baptism there will be women. It'll soon be time for you to choose a good wife."

I kept digging. The sound of the shovel scraping the dirt was not loud enough to drown out Dad's voice.

"Yeah, you son of a bitch," I thought to myself, "you want to get me in even deeper. You want to trap me; bury me in it. Well, you son of a bitch, what you don't know is that it's not going to happen 'cause I'm not doing any of this. I don't want an Amish woman with hairy legs and above all I don't want to be Amish. This is bull shit. If I need to dig a trench I will get a trencher, put it in the ground and operate it myself. It would be so much easier. Instead I'm breaking my back out in the hot sun and this digging has absolutely nothing to do with God! Here he is, the powerful Bishop, thinking this is God's way. What is his damn problem?"

I knew I was playing with fire and I understood I had to control my anger or I would be severely punished. Experience taught me that if you were stupid enough to get a lashing, you deserved the pain and humiliation that resulted. Unfortunately, I was satisfied neither with avoiding confrontations nor keeping my differences a secret. I was incapable of a peaceful coexistence: I was driven!

I continued to "break the rules." I chewed tobacco and seized every opportunity that came my way to disobey Dad. As long as I kept quiet and didn't get caught I was OK.

Dad continued speaking. I had to listen even though I tried to shut him out. I kept digging despite the suffocating heat. It was something to do while his voice droned on.

Dad said, "We have witnessed the fall of many Amish people in different communities. Some of them chose to take a defiant stand. They're young, bold and ignorant, and you are seriously starting to remind me of them. They neither know the Lord nor understand His ways. As a result they are always disturbed and let their tempers control them. Working with your hands is the Lord's way. 'In the sweat of your brow you shall eat bread,' Dad quoted."

"Christy, these words are written in the Bible. We must obey the Lord's wishes."

I listened in silence. It was pointless to argue with Dad. We continued digging until the trench was completed.

❋ ❋ ❋

At forty, Uncle Ralph Burkholder was diagnosed with colon cancer. He refused to believe his time had come and he was being summoned by the Lord. He did not feel ready to leave his family, denied his gloomy fate and chose to explore his options, seeking medical treatment at the hospital. He heeded the 'English' doctor's advice to undergo a surgical procedure as part of his treatment.

Uncle Ralph had a colostomy hopeful the operation would halt the spread of cancer and prolong his life.

"Christy," Dad said, "Uncle Ralph agreed to surgery. He feels he's too young to die and wants to be with his family awhile longer. However, when the Lord summons we must go willingly. Refusing to obey the Will of God leads to a lot of pain and anguish."

Dad was right. Uncle Ralph suffered terribly as a result of the disabling procedure. Shortly before his agony came to an end, he admitted regretting his decision, admitting the pain and misery outweighed the benefits. His condition was humiliating and confining, compromising the quality of his life.

One Sunday after Church service Jacob Yoder, a tall pigeon-toed young folk, and Eve Mast, a short, plump dumb-witted girl, were summoned to come forward.

"It has come to my attention," the Bishop announced, "that Jacob Yoder and Eve Mast are unfit individuals in the community."

Since I was seventeen and had not officially embraced the Amish faith, I was not permitted to attend the special meeting open only to Baptized members. However, I later learned that Jacob and Eve, who was pregnant with his child, were condemned to burn in hell for their sin.

Jacob hurriedly exited Church. His face was pale and his expression somber. Eve remained behind since the service was held in her parents' house. Jacob hitched the buggy and drove away at a reckless pace. The crunching of gravel under his careening wheels was a prelude to the clouds of dust he left behind.

"Yep," I said to William after the service, "Jacob and Eve got kicked out of Church!"

The couple could not be married in the Amish Tradition because they were condemned for their evil deed. Their punishment involved a six month period in which they were forbidden to have any contact with each other. The only way they could gain back the graces lost through sin and receive the Lord's pardon was by attending Church. However, they were shunned by their parents and forced to eat alone in a corner of the room. Despite the mortification, they knew that if they failed to attend Sunday Service they would face a prolonged sentence.

I was infuriated and did not understand why Jacob and Eve had to face public humiliation and eat in an isolated angle of the room in front of everyone. Although I knew better, I questioned why they couldn't just be asked to leave before dinner. Humiliation was part of the learning process. Without the pain and anxiety of shame and dishonor a lesson could not be learned.

After the six month sentence had been served, the couple was permitted to exchange their marriage vows, without the fanfare of a traditional wedding ceremony. Finally Jacob Yoder and Eve Mast became husband and wife.

I continued to disregard Dad's rules, even though he seemed intent on ignoring me whenever possible. I snipped my hair above my ears after Dad had given me a bowl haircut and rolled up my shirt sleeves beyond my elbows while doing chores. These seemingly harmless actions were considered bold and strictly forbidden because uncovering the upper arm showed the configuration of the muscles whenever the arm moved.

Creating a self-image was taboo in the Old Order Amish Tradition. Modesty was preached; therefore the body was to be kept covered beneath long, loose garments. All photographs were banned. No one would ever pose for or snap a picture of another Amish individual. Taking pictures was an 'English' custom which carried the penalty of eternal damnation.

By this time, most of the rules seemed ridiculous to me. I had one main objective; to irritate Dad. Since I was the Bishop's son, my bold deeds and wrong doings caused him much embarrassment and humiliation. I on the other hand enjoyed the power I acquired to anger and upset him.

One evening, several days later, my sister Rebecca informed me that Wilma Beachy, a fourteen year old girl, had given birth to a baby fathered by her brother who was now 'English.' Rebecca heard the news at a Special Meeting in Church. These meetings were strictly confidential. Any serious discussions that took place and all rules formulated pertaining to the Old Order Amish Tradition were kept top secret.

Rebecca's disclosure surprised me.

I asked, "Is it true? Did Wilma Beachy have a baby at fourteen?" Elma was seated nearby and looked at Rebecca with an interested expression on her face.

"Yeah, Christy," Rebecca said, "Wilma and her brother were playing out in the hay mow and I guess something evil happened. He's now 'English' and going to hell."

I thought to myself, "A brother and sister having a baby is a bad thing. It makes sense that he would be going to hell."

However, I disliked Rebecca's insistence that he was condemned because he was 'English.' I hated the hypocrisy and absurd judgments and held Dad guilty on both counts. His duplicitous personality irritated me beyond endurance, especially when he spoke of forgiveness.

I remember the day Uncle Edwin boasted about a snake in his pocket, while putting up hay, to convey his sexual potency. When I mentioned this evil deed to Dad, he reacted oddly.

"Christy," he said, "Uncle Edwin is weak. You know it's not right to dwell on the failings of others. Christy, we must be forgiving!"

I stared at Dad, quickly turned on my heels and walked away.

"You think you know all about forgiving," I muttered to myself, furious; "You back-stabbing son of a bitch! You tell me to forgive Uncle Edwin yet you are incapable of forgiving the people who have fallen away from the Amish Tradition. And what about the young folks and children you brutally beat instead of forgiving! Why don't you practice the rules you preach? Well, if Uncle Edwin can do bad things and get away with it so can I!"

I now realized who Dad was, having unmasked the hypocrisy that suffocated his credibility.

A tumult raged within me; I was angry and I was disgusted. However, I now knew the score would be settled. His time would come: Soon it would be his turn to taste the same bitter pain and humiliation he forced on others.

❋ ❋ ❋

Chapter 14

I was disobedient and rebellious, seeking to alleviate my frustrations and avenge the pain and humiliation I suffered as a result of "breaking Dad's rules." My rampages earned me the title of "outlaw" and I was proud of my evil deeds. As the Bishop's son, my wrong doings were more severe because I brought scorn to a powerful authority figure in the Amish Tradition. I knew my days in the community were now limited and watching Dad lose the power I always coveted led me to reassess my personal goals. However, tangled in my own anger and confusion, I still believed I could resolve my dilemmas through brutal and aggressive actions. Sadly, I was not any better than the very person I disliked and disrespected: Dad.

Dad seemed to have changed his attitude towards me. His "turn the other cheek" philosophy was a different approach from the double hand slaps and chain hobbles beatings I received in the past. My mischievous deeds were now handled with a warning and soon forgotten. Dad would verbally discipline me then turn on his heels and walk away. He was unsure of his power over me and felt his authority slip. I instead felt a surge of power; the power I had always envied.

My sister Rebecca met a young man who had asked for her hand in marriage. I was excited and thrilled, believing I would finally be rid of her. She would be moving to another house in the settlement and I felt relieved. I had received a reprieve from her conniving intrigues and spiteful tattling!

It was a brisk clear morning, and Rebecca's wedding was scheduled for the following day. The chilly temperatures gave evidence winter was approaching. Since the guest list included the wild bunch from Bowling Green, I knew I had to buy my own whiskey or risk being called a chicken shit for mooching a drink from the others.

At seventeen I was finally old enough to join the young folks gathering on the wedding night. This get-together was always considered an important event. There was laughing, singing and friendly socializing. Even though the Elders were often present, it was customary for the young folks to reunite in the barn to drink and smoke. I knew I had to have my own liquor if I didn't want to be mocked. I drew up a plan and set it in motion.

Dad allowed me to train a horse for the 'English' neighbor as a pastime after my chores were completed. This offered me a good excuse to wear my knee high rubber boots without drawing unnecessary attention when I was training the horse.

I dressed myself and headed over to the barn. I mounted my horse and galloped over to St. Francisville, a tiny town near the Des Moines River. Three miles into the ride, I came to the gas station, dismounted and walked in.

The previous evening, while Dad slept, I had snuck down to the living room on my toes not daring to breathe for fear of waking him or Mom. Reaching the desk, I opened the drawer, picked up his wallet and took out a ten dollar bill. I folded it in half, put it in my pocket and restored the wallet to its original place. It felt good to have this amount of money safely hidden under my coat.

"I'll take a pint of Kessler Whiskey," I said to the sales clerk, feeling important. I was excited to be purchasing liquor. It was my first time and I tried to seem like I knew what I was doing.

"Do you have any ID with you?" The clerk responded, extending her hand. "I have to check your ID before I can give you the whiskey."

"I don't have any," I said, looking her straight in the eye. "I'm Amish!"

ID? I had no idea what she was talking about.

From across the counter she chuckled, obviously entertained by my comment and puzzled expression. She did not insist.

"That'll be six dollars," she said, casting me an amused glance.

"Great," I thought to myself. "I got my whiskey and I have enough money left over to buy a pack of cigarettes!"

After paying for the whiskey and cigarettes, I went outside, feeling lucky the woman did not insist on seeing my "ID." Clutching the whiskey tightly, I held it firmly against my stomach, under my coat until I was out of her view.

Bending over, I rolled up my pant leg and stuck the whisky down the side of my boot. The bottle slid down my leg, stopping at my ankle bone. I then lowered my pant leg. The bottle created quite an unusual bulge and I hoped it would not be noticed before I was back at the barn and able to hide it.

As the horse galloped, the bottle slid up and down my leg. The continual friction against my skin caused a painful blister right on my ankle bone. However, I felt having the whiskey was well worth the gnawing discomfort. Nothing could dampen my high spirits. Tomorrow was Rebecca's wedding. She would be gone from my life and I had whiskey and cigarettes to celebrate the occasion. It couldn't get any better.

I neared the barn, rode over to the buggy shed and quickly fastened the horse. I hid the whisky on top of a wide ceiling beam. The cigarettes I stashed further down just in case Dad discovered the whiskey. This way I was assured of securing either the liquor or the cigarettes. For years I had heard the young folks caution against putting all your treasures in one spot.

I was well equipped and prepared for Rebecca's wedding and the events that followed. I sat calmly at supper that evening.

"Christy," Dad said. "Many people will be coming for Rebecca's wedding. I don't want any ruckus or disturbances to spoil the day. Just obey the rules you've been taught. You know what is right and what is expected of you. This will be a humble wedding in keeping with the Amish Tradition."

Early the following morning, the guests started to arrive and by nine o'clock the house was filled to capacity. Additional guests were received in the basement where a Bishop from a different community and several Preachers greeted them and delivered the sermons.

Old Order Amish weddings are simple and modest in keeping with tradition. Neither floral arrangements nor music are used during the service and no pictures are taken. Although the setting is somber and devoid of any flourish, a joyful spirit prevails.

Mom and Dad had approved of Rebecca's fiancé, Andy, the banns announcing the marriage had been published in Church and the ceremony was scheduled.

When everyone was seated, Rebecca and Andy entered the house. They walked to the front of the congregation where the Bishop and Preachers waited for them, stood opposite each other for a brief second and took their seats. Their wedding would be the first and last occasion in which they would sit together during a service.

In the Old Order Amish Tradition men and women neither prayed nor worshiped in the same room in Church. The men remained in the living room while the women retreated to the kitchen.

The witnesses, two couples, entered and seated themselves; the boys on one side and the girls on the other. The Preacher cleared his throat.

"This is a joyful day," he announced. "Two more young people from the flock have accepted the Lord's way. They have come together in a proper and dignified manner, uniting their lives, humbly and meekly in accordance with God's Will. The Lord will accompany them throughout their journey on earth."

Marriage is the turning point for Old Order Amish young folks. Once a woman is married she keeps her vow to love, honor and obey until death do us part. They remain in a submissive position, accepting their husband's rule, fully complying with his wishes, never daring to disagree or contradict either his decisions or actions.

Since the Bishop alone is vested with the power and authority to perform a marriage rite, it was Rebecca's request that Dad unite her and Andy.

After the service was concluded and before the last song was sung, Rebecca and Andy were asked to come forward.

"Andy and Rebecca," Dad said, "do you agree in the name of the Lord to continue serving the Church?"

"Yes, we do," Rebecca and Andy answered in unison.

"Andy and Rebecca, do you agree to live a long virtuous life in the Lord's favor according to the Amish Tradition?"

"Yes, we do," the couple responded. Their faces glowed with excitement as they waited eagerly for Dad to administer their vows.

After Rebecca and Andy pronounced their "I dos" agreeing to take each other as their respective mates, until death, they promised their reciprocal love, respect and fidelity. Rebecca, in keeping with tradition, promised to obey Andy. After the vows were spoken, they were united in the presence of God.

"I now pronounce you man and wife through the Lord."

A song was sung and the couple went outside followed by the four witnesses and the young folks. The ceremony was followed by a light lunch, quickly prepared by the women.

Later that evening I took the whiskey I stashed in the barn and drank with the other boys. Intoxicated, I returned to the house as the guests were beginning to depart. I had stuffed my mouth with gum to camouflage the aroma of whiskey on my breath.

"Christy," Dad said, as I stumbled inside, "have you been drinking?"

"No, Dad," I said and headed for the stairs. Dad gave me a questioning look, but did not pursue the matter. It was a serene conclusion.

I remember the day William, Cousins Will and Paul and I

decided to go sparrow hunting on Jeff Murray's property while he and his wife were vacationing in Texas.

Excited, I said to the boys, "I'm going to get the key from Jeff's shed."

"What for?" William said.

Without pausing to respond, I headed for the shed, took the key, opened Jeff's door and entered his house. A few minutes later, I stepped out, dangling the truck keys.

"Instead of sparrow hunting," I said, proudly, "we're going for a ride!"

Ruthless and no longer afraid, I took the wheel. I slammed my foot on the accelerator; the motor choked and raced. I watched in awe as the speedometer climbed to sixty miles an hour. My pulse raced. The tires of the truck crunched the stones and gravel along the road, leaving clouds of dust as evidence of my evil deed. The truck vibrated and jumped every time I drove over a bump in the road. I had the power to make this vehicle run! I felt proud and exhilarated. Speed was thrilling but power was awesome!

I indulged in several forbidden pleasures and broke some pretty severe rules, enjoying the feeling. Fear of condemnation was no longer my guardian. I looked for more occasions to disobey. Rebellious and defiant, at seventeen, the Bishop's son was charting his own course. I continued to seek enjoyment through forbidden adventures.

Amos Mast was an older young folk, disliked for his insufferable personality. He hung with a group of boys who often disobeyed the rules. One evening, I walked outside behind the barn and found Amos and his friends smoking cigarettes.

"Hey Amos," I said, "can I have a cigarette?" I had my own pack sitting in my pocket, but was apprehensive about admitting it in front of these boys. They had their own gang which was almost impossible to infiltrate. I knew they did not accept me in their group; therefore I was cautious about revealing anything they could use against me. Instead, I preferred to smoke my own cigarettes with my friends, Petie and Wilmer Eicher, certain they would not tattle on me.

Wilmer was an overgrown boy, four years older than me, with dark hair and eyes, who laughed almost as much as he lied. His brother Petie was a tall, stocky seventeen year old with a reckless nature, blonde bushy hair, blue eyes and exaggeratedly long arms. He had a rather nonchalant attitude and detached approach to life but, like his brother, he laughed a lot.

"Christy," Amos said, "I'll give you a severe whipping, if you tell anyone you saw us smoking."

"Look, Amos," I said, "if you sons of bitches can smoke, so can I."

"Well, Christy," Amos said without removing the cigarette from his mouth, "since we haven't been caught, I guess we can trust you." He reached into his pocket and pulled out a pack of cigarettes.

"You sons of bitches," I said, pulling a pack from my pocket, "I don't want your damn cigarettes. I've got my own."

Grasping the pack with my right hand, I slapped it against my left index finger. A cigarette popped up. I slid it out, positioned it between my lips, lit it, took a long drag and exhaled a cloud of smoke directly in his face. Amos stood motionless except for his eyes. He turned his glance on the other boys. His furrowed brow betrayed his anger. No one said a word.

"I showed him," I thought, feeling proud. "I had the courage to stand up to Amos and his gang of older young folks. I made him look like an idiot," I chuckled. "He was an older boy, and I got him to offer me one of his cigarettes, then I refused it." I felt cool and pleased with myself. The idea that they trusted me was exciting.

I was reluctant to tell William about my smoking with the older boys. He still tattled on me at times and often seemed to enjoy when I got in trouble. To settle the score, whenever I had an opportunity I'd try to pull one over on him.

One day I was upset with him over his continual insistence that he always milked more cows than I did. It was Saturday, and the day set aside for weekly bathing. Mom and Dad had already bathed and the water had been changed for my sisters, William and me. After Elma and Tina were finished, it was my turn to bathe. William was the last. Tina was one year younger than me and Mom and Dad's fourth child. After my bath I took the hot water still on the burner and poured it down the drain, to prevent him from having enough to change the dirty water. I returned back to the tub, climbed in, pooped and got out, laughing to myself. The poop floated around a bit and sunk beneath the dark grey soap bubbles.

"William will never notice anything," I thought to myself, "until he's sitting in the tub. Then it'll be too late." I chuckled and went upstairs. Later, after his bath, William came into the bedroom, looking disturbed. I controlled my urge to laugh out loud.

He said, "You son of a bitch. You shit in the tub, didn't you?"

"Yeah, William," I said, "how do you like soaking in my poop? Well, let that be a lesson. Don't you ever mess with me again." I gave him a stern look and he understood I meant what I said.

I wanted to be a free person and I would stop anyone who dared to thwart my wishes. I knew I still had a long road ahead, but I was willing and able to do whatever was necessary to achieve my goal.

❋ ❋ ❋

Chapter 15

I was becoming more independent, although I was not yet mature enough to steer my own life. I turned my back on the world of silent suffering and began to vocalize my feelings and thoughts, standing up to Dad and crushing the power he exercised over me. This confrontational strategy reversed the roles, giving me a bit of the power I always coveted. Once I tasted the fruit of authority, I questioned if achieving this power was my key to self-gratification. Uncertainties and qualms sprung and I had misgivings about the true value of power. Perhaps I needed to step beyond the acquisition of control to attain my real goal: Maybe the secret to happiness was not power, but freedom! It was a new idea to explore.

In the Old Order Amish Tradition large families are quite common. Birth control is unheard of and a woman's main purpose in life is to bare children. The sole focus of sexual intercourse is procreation, therefore once a man's wife becomes pregnant, the couple's sexual act has been blessed. During the pregnancy, the husband is obliged to abstain from any sexual activity with his wife until after the birth of the baby.

Late one evening I heard Mom was not feeling very well. She was expecting another child and had not presented herself at the supper table for two consecutive evenings, preferring to remain in her room.

Suddenly around ten o'clock Mom's piercing screams broke the evening stillness. I was startled. My heart raced as the terrifying cries continued. It seemed as if someone was beating her.

"Elma," I said to my sister, running into her room, "what's wrong with Mom? Why is she screaming?"

"Christy," she whispered, "I think Mom's gonna have a baby."

I said, "Where's that lady who delivers babies?"

"You mean the mid-wife, Christy?" Elma said.

"Yeah," I said, "that lady."

"Well, uh, I don't know, Christy," she said.

Mom continued to scream. I was upset by her cries. An hour later I approached Elma, Tina and William again.

"I'm going downstairs, to see how Mom's doing," I said. "I can't stand to hear her scream like that. Something's gotta be wrong."

"No, Christy," William said, "Dad will take care of it." By now William had become quite close knit with Dad. He was obedient and Dad believed he had succeeded in raising a good son who respected him as well as the Lord and the Amish Tradition.

I insisted Mom needed help and went downstairs followed by Elma, Tina and William. We huddled together in the living room which was adjacent to Mom and Dad's bedroom. The screaming became louder and more piercing. Mom's bed rattled and squeaked. I held my breath and asked the Lord to relieve her misery. Just as I whispered "amen" I heard the shrill cry of an infant.

Dad came out with our new born sister in his arms. The baby seemed so tiny wrapped in a big blanket. Her tear stained face was pink and contorted. She was gasping and crying, expanding her lungs to full capacity. Dad instead was ashen. Shiny beads of sweat ran down his cheeks, sliding into his beard.

"Look!" he said, excited, "This is Rachel, your new sister." He was so proud.

Dad set Rachel down on the table, opened the bulky blanket

and freed her face. He bent over her little body, inserted in her mouth a plastic apparatus similar to one used by doctors and aspirated the fluid that was blocking her air passage. When he was assured she was breathing properly, Dad brought Rachel back to Mom. He returned to the living room several minutes later, not expecting to see us still standing around discussing our new sister.

In the Old Order Amish Tradition, newborns were not immunized against many of the serious childhood illnesses since oral medications were the only acceptable remedy for curing illnesses.

My gazed slipped to Dad's hand. I noticed he carried a bottle of Mogen David, a liturgical wine used in Church exclusively for Communion. When he spotted us, he tried to hide the bottle behind his back with a quick swing of his arm.

The bottle was half empty and judging from Dad's pasty complexion and the far-away look in his eyes I knew he had been drinking.

"Everything is fine," Dad said.

"Yeah, you son of a bitch," I said to myself; "everything is just fine and dandy 'cause once again you played God! Mom was in agony. She screamed and cried for over two and a half hours while you just stood there drinking the wine. Now you have the nerve to come in here satisfied and proud of yourself."

I was enraged. I felt a different anger towards Dad. It was more intense and penetrating. I turned and darted up the stairs. Dad continued to carry Rachel around the house, showing her off to Elma, William and Tina.

No one ever dared to contradict Dad. No one ever had the courage to stand up to him, either in defense of an unjust accusation or to accuse him of a wrong doing. He was the Bishop and he inspired fear in his family and in his flock: Dad could do no wrong. Yet while Mom screamed in pain, he sat drinking Communion wine instead of getting medical assistance to ease her pain. I was disgusted and wanted no part of him or his hypocritical ways.

I continued to work for Jeff Murray, often helping him put up hay. While in his shop one day, I spotted his radio. I walked over to where it sat and looked around to see if he was watching. Certain he was busy elsewhere, I snatched it. At the end of the day when Jack locked up, I hid the radio outside the barn. Later that evening, I returned to pick it up and hid it in the hay mow. I was excited and proud of myself.

The following morning when Jeff unlocked the shop, he noticed the radio was missing.

"Chris," he said, "did you see my little radio while you were working in the shed?"

"No, Mr. Murray," I lied, "I didn't see any radio." Jack dismissed the issue and no further mention was made.

After chores I climbed the hay mow, rummaged through the hay, uncovered the radio and listened curiously to the various transmissions.

One evening I invited William to the barn.

I said, "Let's climb the hay mow."

"What for, Christy?" he said, always questioning my actions.

"Just shut up and follow me," I replied. "You'll see."

When we reached the top of the hay mow, I pushed aside some of the hay, and pulled out the radio. I turned it on at low volume.

"That's a radio, isn't it?" William said, wide eyed, His face was flushed with excitement.

"Yeah, William," I replied. "Sure it's a radio. Shhh, listen. People talk and then there's music and singing."

"O, Christy," he said holding his breath, "we'd better not get caught. Dad will give us a severe beating if he finds out we have a radio!"

"No, William," I said, "we better not get caught. If Dad finds out you'll be in just as much trouble as I will."

"Don't worry, Christy," William said, "I promise I won't say anything."

That Sunday morning the girls decided to walk the mile and a half to Church. I preferred to take the buggy. I was proud that

I had built it myself and I wanted to show off Diamond, my long-legged black stallion with a white diamond on his face.

I went out to the barn and after I hitched up Diamond, I walked over to where my radio was hidden. William followed in my footsteps, curious to see what I was up to.

"William," I said, showing him the radio, "I'm going to take this radio upstairs. I'd like to listen to it at night and I don't want to have to pretend to poop to come out here."

William said, "Where did you get the radio?"

"I took it from Jeff Murray's shop," I said.

"Does Mr. Murray know you took it?" William said.

"No," I said. "He asked me if I had seen it. When I said no, he believed me."

"Christy," William answered, "I don't think it's smart to take the radio into the house."

"Well, William," I said, "it doesn't make a difference what you think."

"Well, Christy," he said, "I'm not gonna take it anywhere!"

"You don't have to," I said, "I'll do it. Just pull the buggy from the shed and wait for me."

Amish people did not own radios. It was looked upon as sinful to either have one or listen to one.

Despite an almost paralyzing fear of getting caught, I was determined to bring the radio upstairs.

Once in my bedroom, I looked for a safe hiding place. Walking over to my closet, I shoved the radio under some things stored on the top shelf.

"No one will ever find it up here," I whispered to myself.

Every evening, William and I continued to turn on the radio at a low volume. We enjoyed the transmissions and above all the music.

One evening while we listened, Dad suddenly opened the door. The light from the lamp he carried flickered in the darkness of the room casting a beam of light on my face. Hearing his footsteps on the stairs and the creak of the door as it swung open, William and I quickly moved our pillows and pretended to be asleep.

"Boys!" Dad said.

"Yeeeah," I said, pretending his entry had wakened me from a deep sleep. I rubbed my eyes, yawned widely and waited for his next words.

"Boys," Dad said, "I was on my way up the stairs and I thought I heard some sounds. Is there a mouse squeaking?"

I said, "I didn't hear anything. I don't think there's a mouse in here, 'cause if there was something William and I would have heard it."

I took a deep breath when Dad walked out the door.

"William, "I said, "That was a close call. We almost got caught. I've got to think of something."

Soon after, while rummaging though a dumpster, I found a pair of earphones. It was a perfect solution. William and I shared the ear piece, each of us listening to the radio with one ear.

"Christy, William," Dad said one evening after supper, "why don't you sit down here any more and read?"

I said, "There are no interesting books to read. There's only the Bible!"

"Christy," he said, his gaze stern, "what's wrong with reading the Bible?"

"Well," I said, turning to head upstairs, "nothing, I suppose."

"William," Dad said, "stay down here a moment. I'd like to talk to you."

Dad was certain he had heard something in our room and was determined to resolve the mystery. When William came up later that evening he was anxious and nervous.

"Christy," he said, "Dad suspects something. He asked me if I know anything about a radio."

"What did you say, William?" I said, my heart racing.

"Nothing, Christy," he said. "I told Dad we come up here and just talk and maybe read sometimes."

I chuckled at William's attempts to cover up our naughty action.

Dad did not accept William's explanation and continued to suspect something was not quite right. From the change in our behavior, he knew we were trying to conceal some mischievous deed.

One day at lunch time, I went out to the barn to poop and Dad cornered William.

"Christy," William said when I came out, "Dad knows we have the radio."

"What do you mean?" I said. "How did he find out?" I knew I was in serious trouble and felt my stomach flip.

William said, "He told me he saw it."

"What did you say to Dad?" I said.

"I told him, yeah, we've got a radio."

"William," I said, feeling my anger rise, "you must be the dumbest, most stupid idiot alive. You told Dad we have a radio! He was pulling your damn leg and you fell for it. How could you let him trick you?"

William said, "I didn't know what to say. He told me he saw it."

"Did he show it to you?" I said. "You dumb ass. Was he holding the radio in his hands?"

"No, Christy, he didn't show it to me."

"Well, did he tell you he knew where it was?" I said, not daring to breathe.

"Nnno, nooo, Christy," he answered, beginning to stutter.

"You lying idiot," I said. "You gave me your word you wouldn't tell Dad about the radio. I've had it, William, I'm done. I'm sick and tired of you and your dumb nonsense. Dad will whip the shit out of me, 'cause you're a stupid little boy who can't keep his mouth shut." Angered, I left the barn.

When I came in the house, I noticed Dad standing near the kitchen door. His face was ashen and his brow knitted in deep wrinkles. His breathing seemed shallow and labored. I knew he was upset. He glared at me in a cold, odd way.

"Christy," he said, "do you know anything about a radio?"

"Yeah, Dad," I said, "I've had one for quite some time now."

"Yyyou what?" he said, "Wwwhat dddo you mean?"

At this point I realized it was senseless to deny my wrong

doing. I admitted having the radio and was prepared for my punishment. The quicker I was beaten, the sooner it would be over with.

Dad walked up to me, clutching the radio.

"It's this, isn't it?" he said, "waving the radio in my face. "Yes, Dad," I said, ducking as he approached. "That's the radio."

Dad said, "After all my teachings about following the 'English' and the bad consequences you would face, you defied my rules." He slammed the radio on the cook stove, lifted it and crushed it with his bear hands. He looked wild and I was terrified.

"Come downstairs, Christy," he said. Dad's hands were trembling; his face was pale and his breathing heavy. His foul breath hit me in the face. I backed up and fixed my gaze on the floor. I feared something more serious than usual was about to happen.

Once downstairs, Dad turned sharply to face me. He grasped my shoulder. I winced as his jagged nails cut into my flesh.

"Christy," he said, "I don't know what to do with you. You leave me no choice but to beat you."

"Dad," I said, "you've been whipping, slapping and beating me all my life. So what's different this time?"

"What, Christy?" Dad said, "Now you're getting mouthy and defiant with me. What's wrong with you, Christy? I must have missed something. The devil has taken possession of your spirit! That radio is the devil's tool!"

I refused any eye contact and continued to stare down at my feet.

"Christy, you leave me no choice." Dad yelled freeing his grasp on my shoulder. He indicated with his icy stare, the direction in which he wanted me to go. "Go over there and stand up near that post," he said.

I knew I would have to grind my teeth and grip the post with all my strength. Dad was infuriated and I was certain he would give me a vicious beating.

Dad walked over to the counter near the window. Too terrified to move, I followed him with my eyes. He searched around looking for a weapon and removed a piece of baling wire, hanging from a nail. It was a tightly wound circular loop about three feet long.

"Christy," Dad said, shoving the wire in my face, "do you realize what I'm going to do?"

"Whatever," I said. I knew the situation at this point was hopeless anyway.

"Whatever!" he repeated as he started to beat me. He hit me across my butt, working his way up to my back and shoulders. Dad forcefully lifted the baling wire in the air before bringing it down on his target. He was silent but had a wild gaze I had never seen before. All his energy was concentrated in his right arm which gripped and swung the baling wire. His scowl betrayed his obsession with violence. Dad was merciless and absorbed by the power he believed he still had over me, denying the inevitable: He struggled frantically, to defend the control he knew was slipping out of his reach.

I clenched my teeth as the wire flew through the air announcing its arrival on my back. I cringed; the pain was excruciating. My shirt clung to my skin. I was bleeding and on fire. My wounds burned and itched. My anger raged.

"Is that enough, Christy?" Dad said dropping the baling wire to the ground. The thud of the weapon hitting the floor did little to either ease my pain or calm the resentment, disgust and hatred I felt towards Dad.

"Did you hear me, Christy?" Dad continued, unsatisfied with my silence. "Did you have enough or do you need more?"

"Whatever," I said. "It doesn't really make a difference 'cause this is the last time you're gonna beat me. Now did you hear what I said?"

"Christy," he said, "I'm going to beat you some more. You're defiant and you refuse to learn."

"Go ahead," I said without blinking an eye. "Go right ahead and beat me all you want. Enjoy the whipping, Dad, 'cause this is your last chance to see me bleed. After this you will never touch me again."

I released my grip from the post and although I was numb from the lashings, I felt a warm flow of blood trickle down my back.

"You will never touch me again," I shouted, turning to face him. I pointed my finger at him and yelled, "I hope you enjoyed it, 'cause this is it. This is the last time you beat me."

Stunned, Dad lowered his gaze. He was trembling. I saw a different man, a weak fearful man whom I had never seen before. In silence he turned, took several hesitant and unsteady steps and went upstairs.

William came back down. He had already been beaten for listening to the radio and not confessing to Dad.

"O, man" William said, "Dad was sure yelling at you."

"Yeah, William," I said, turning away from him. "Take a look at my back!"

"O My God," William said, shocked. "Christy, you're bleeding. Your shirt is covered with blood. Man, that's gotta hurt."

"Yeah, William," I said. "It hurts! He nailed me good, that son of a bitch!"

"Well, Christy," William said, "I guess Dad had to whip you, but he certainly didn't have to be so brutal."

"Yeah, William," I said, "Dad thinks he's God. He thinks he can do whatever he damn pleases and get away with it."

I tried to take a deep breath. The pain was agonizing. I had to suffer because the Bishop had to prove his power and control.

"William," I said, "get a towel. Do you hear me? Go get me a damn towel!" The numbness had subsided, substituted by a burning soreness that intensified with every breath I took.

By the time William arrived with the towel I was riddled with unbearable pain. The baling wire had cut through my skin, ripping it wide open.

"Man, Christy," he said when he saw my torn bloody flesh. "Dad must have been really brutal his time. Your back is a mess!"

Suddenly we heard the door slam as Dad walked into the room. I locked eyes with him for the first time in my life. My icy stare was bred of anger, hate and disgust. It was a resentful gaze filled with years of silent suffering, hidden frustrations and controlled reprisals. Dad lowered his gaze unable to meet my eyes.

"Christy, are you OK?" he said.

"What does it matter to you," I said. "You never cared how I felt. Don't tell me you suddenly care!"

Dad turned and left the room in silence. I never again felt his wrath on my skin. The Bishop had delivered his last beating: His power over me was lost.

"That son of a bitch knows I'll hit him square between the eyes if he ever touches me again," I said, "I'll knock him right off his feet. I don't care anymore."

I continued sobbing from the physical pain, the emotional hurt and the agonizing wounds of the past that never healed. The Bishop's first born son was lost.

One afternoon, not long after, William failed to present himself at the lunch table. Dad was concerned by his absence.

"I'm going back out to the field," Dad said, "I want to see what's keeping William. He's usually here at lunchtime."

After Dad left, I took a big dip of chew and tied to flatten it out without getting caught. Suddenly I heard the heavy clip-clops of a horse at full gallop. Dad had returned.

"Christy," he shouted, "get Red hitched up! Hurry, hook him up to the buggy and get the handyman jack."

The handyman jack was a tool utilized to raise heavy objects. It stood five feet tall and had a hook at the base which moved up when the handle was pumped.

"What's wrong, Dad?" I said almost gagging on the chew in my mouth. I turned my head and spit it out before Dad realized I was chewing.

"William's had a nasty accident." He got his foot caught in the disk."

Dad and I rushed out to the field together. He drove Red at break-neck speed while I held firm to the back of the buggy, struggling to keep from bouncing out. I feared for William knowing the disk was extremely heavy.

When we arrived we spotted William. He was yelling in pain.

"Dad! Dad! Hurry! My foot hurts!"

William had swung his bare foot into the center of the disk, where the ten inch blades rotated continually. The force yanked him from the seat before he could halt the team of horses. Although he immediately shouted, "Whoa, whoa," the horses did not stop instantly. As a result, William was dragged up to his knees under the disk and trapped for an hour and a half in a seated position. With the raw steel bar frame of the disk settled between his legs, he was uncomfortable. His right foot was bloody and sliced to the bone. With the help of the handyman jack, Dad relieved the tension, freed William's foot and carried him to the buggy. He was shaking and sobbing, looking down at his mangled foot. The bone had pierced through his skin, tearing the flesh. The scene was frightful and it was clear from William's wide-eyed stare that he was terrified.

When we arrived at the barn Dad mixed a solution of kerosene, water and rubbing alcohol which he applied to William's wounded foot.

"Dad," I said, feeling queasy and uneasy about William's injury; "Why don't you take him to the doctor?" William was trembling and obviously in shock.

"No, Christy," Dad said. "We can handle this ourselves. I know what I'm doing. William will be OK!"

Dad was right. Eventually William's foot healed without serious physical consequences although the accident left him morally shaken.

Several days later, after lunch, William sat down with Dad.

"Dad," he said, "I've been sitting here, thinking a lot and I understand what happened."

"What do you mean, William?" Dad said.

"Well, Dad, I did some bad things and the Lord punished me."

"What did you do William?" Dad asked setting down his book.

William lowered his eyes, sighed and said, "Dad I need to confess."

"OK, William," he said, "Tell me what's wrong."

"Dad," William said staring down at his hands folded in his lap, "I had sex with the cows, I smoked cigarettes and I helped Christy hide the radio. We listened to it together and I never tried to stop him from turning it on. I enjoyed listening to the music just as much as he did."

"Well, William," Dad said, "I see you have learned your lesson. Yes, you have done evil things and the Lord has punished you." He took a deep breath and continued.

"The Lord stopped you when I was unable to see what was happening. William, you must ask the Lord to forgive your wrongs. Tell Him you'll repent your evil ways and live a better life following the rules I've taught you."

"Yes, Dad, I will," William said, crying. He felt relieved of his burden.

Although William's conscience had been cleared, he was vulnerable and susceptible to Dad's teachings. The horror and pain surrounding the Lord's punishment left an enduring impression on him. It was all about fear, guilt and the dire consequences of sin. It was ingrained in us and we were expected to live it. Still today, William remains a strict religious Old Order Amish, held firm to the Tradition by an almost paralyzing, all consuming fear of eternal condemnation.

I understood I could no longer count on William to be my accomplice. Dad had crammed him with fear and he was convinced his awful accident was the Lord's way of seeking retribution for his evil doings.

This new violation of trust caused us to grow apart. I knew that if William came to know of any bad deed on my part, he would neither be a willing participant nor close his eyes to my guilt. I felt alone and isolated. Although I was sorry for William's accident, I was enraged with Dad for continuing to intimidate William, filling his head with lies.

My loathing for Dad grew more intense. Yet, despite the hate, sometimes I felt sorry for the power and authority he lost. Other times, however, I considered him a pitiful individual on a hopeless mission. He could no longer bully me into obeying his rules or terrorize me with threats of the Lord's cruel punishment. I understood his power was used strictly for his own benefit and I wanted no part of it. There had to be a more respectable way to achieve happiness and gratification without causing so much pain and agony and I was determined to find it.

❋   ❋   ❋

Chapter 16

It was 1991 and at nineteen, I was expected to assume adult responsibilities in the Amish Tradition. My respect for Dad had turned into a vile contempt driving me to continue my vindictive crusade. His misuse of the power he held as Bishop troubled me. I could rectify neither his thoughts nor his actions. Nothing made any sense. The bitter taste of his outrageous contradictions revolted me. I had turned away from his teachings and rules and found myself seeking to repair my damaged self-esteem and dignity through violent acts. The years of abuse taught me endurance and survival and lead me on a quest to attain my own power.

I questioned the true value of Dad's power and I questioned if power was really something that would make me happy. When wrong doings and an almost sham spirituality invade Church teaching, the struggle to hold on to the tradition becomes meaningless.

One Sunday just before services had ended the Bishop, Elders and Preachers bowed their heads and prayed solemnly. A new disciple was being summoned to the service of the Lord. Disciples are not considered man-appointed. Instead, they are called by the Lord through the Bishop and Elders to serve His flock.

Bishops from other communities would be invited to participate in the ordination of new disciples, offering Dad and the

Preachers additional power and support. It was considered a special gift from the Lord to have this extra sustenance.

Uncle Edwin craved power and was convinced he was chosen by the Lord to be a Preacher. Mom found his idea amusing and we never took him very seriously.

The Elders knelt with their hands clasped tightly in front of their foreheads; their lips were parted in dialogue with the Lord.

"Lord," some whispered, "I will serve you. Please if it is Thy Will I will come forward and be Thy disciple. Lord hear my prayer. I am pleading with Thee to allow me to assume a more important role tending to the Lord's flock."

The prayers of the humble Elders were recited with a different approach.

Through sobs, I heard them whisper, "Lord, I am unworthy to by Thy servant. Please choose my neighbor as Thy humble disciple for he is far more worthy than I to serve Thy flock."

The Bishops retreated to a small room while the members rose to their feet in silence. One of the Bishop's came to the door and motioned for the Elders to come into the room one at a time. He then asked each individual to cast their vote. Although the women members were not permitted to vote, they were summoned to pray for their husbands. After every member cast his vote for the Elder he believed worthy, the Bishops tallied the votes.

It was necessary to receive a minimum of three votes to be seriously considered. The Bishops carried the books, one for each of the seven Elders who had received sufficient votes to qualify as an eligible candidate. The books were piled on the table, one on top of the other while the congregation stared in silence.

Previously, the Bishops had reworded a passage from scripture to fit the election of the new Preacher. It had been handwritten on a slip of paper and inserted in one of the books. The Elder who received the book with the note would be rendered a holy and powerful man.

Dad called the seven men and asked them to come forward and be seated on the bench.

As their names were called each of the Elders stepped forward, removed a book from the top of the stack, and seated himself on the bench. They were crying. Their tears softened the stiffness of their untrimmed beards. When the last man was seated Dad addressed the audience.

"Let us bow our heads in prayer," he said. His expression was stern but reverent. Sniffles, sobs and nose blowing interrupted the dismal quiet. The moment was somber. The Lord was calling a man to His service and the mystery surrounding the chosen Elder was soon to be resolved.

I chuckled silently to myself deriding this sanctimonious practice of God choosing what men had previously voted. Although the process did not make much sense to me, I was curious to see who would be the chosen disciple. I sat, awaiting the revelation.

Dad approached each man one by one, extended his hand and accepted the book offered him by the Elder. He then opened it, turned the pages and searched for the note. It was Uncle Andrew's turn. Dad took his book, opened it and tucked in the crease was a folded piece of paper.

Dad lifted the note and unfolded it.

"Andrew," he said, "you have been chosen."

Uncle Andrew fell to his knees, sobbing. He was hunched over with his head resting on the floor. All eyes focused on his prostrate form as he wept uncontrollably. He was fearful to have been summoned by the Lord!

Dad bent over Uncle Andrew and gently tapped him on the shoulder with his index finger. He then took Uncle Andrew's trembling hand in his.

"You are the Servant of the Lord," Dad proclaimed. "You have hereby received the power of this holy position. You are now able to preach the word of God to the flock."

Dad took a deep breath. "Andrew," he continued, "do you acknowledge the Will of the Lord? Do you accept the Lord's call to help strengthen faith and build the rules in Church? Will you defend the Amish Tradition and no other until death releases you from earthly life and unites you with the Lord?"

"Yes, I do," Uncle Andrew said bursting into another round of fitful crying. The audience sobbed. A new Preacher was ordained, summoned by the Lord to administer the flock. The service ended and Uncle Andrew assumed his new role as Preacher.

Since I bought two twelve packs of beer that evening, there was a generous supply of liquor. Although it was customary for us to drink whiskey, the three girls, including my sister Tina who drank with us on Sunday nights, found the whiskey a bit too strong.

We downed the beer. I was drunk and barely able to stand on my feet. I shuffled into the house, struggling to keep from falling down. When I walked through the door, I found the girls throwing up. They were heaving and gagging. Tina was puking right at the supper table. The stench of undigested food and beer permeated the air. The echo of the girls retching filled the silence. It was a clear attestation of wrong doing.

"We can't deny anything," I thought to myself, "There's blatant evidence we've been drinking."

The community was out of control. By now the young folks were drinking and smoking. At times I felt sorry for Dad. His power was waning.

I tried to sit and eat my supper but the overindulgence upset my stomach.

"The hell with it," I said, pushing my plate away. Witnessing my action and hearing my comment the young folks burst into laughter. The Bishop's son said "hell"!

"What's going on here?" Dad said knitting his brow. "What's all the ruckus about?"

We fell silent and looked at each other with questioning glances.

Once again I felt sorry for Dad. As the Bishop, he believed he had everything under control, yet he was incapable of controlling anything. Although he succeeded momentarily in ending the uproar he was unable to stop it from recurring and ineffective in preventing the drinking. What a confusing and illogical paradox.

"If Dad has so much power," I questioned, "why can't he control the drinking among the young folks?"

"I'm done," I said. Despite Dad's gaze on me, I stood up and walked out. I was surprised to see Petie and Wilmer Eicher, my sister Tina, Cousin Edna and several other young folks boldly rise and follow suit.

"Yeah, we're done," they said.

Once outside, I ran over to my buggy and reached inside to unlock the footboard to get the whiskey I kept hidden. Petie and Wilmer together with the girls and several other boys waited for me in the barn, ready to enjoy a few more drinks.

I noticed the lock had been jammed open and my whiskey was gone. My cigarettes and a small radio I had were also missing. Someone had broken in and stolen my possessions. I was furious. I jumped off the buggy.

"Those sons of bitches," I yelled, "they got my whiskey!" Petie and Wilmer looked at me, their faces ashen.

"No way Christy," Wilmer said.

"How did that happen?" Petie added.

"I don't know," I said, trying to catch my breath, "my lock has been forced open; those sons of bitches. O the hell with it anyway. They're probably out in back of the barn drinking my whiskey. They'll get drunk then come and punish us later, so who gives a damn."

My comment was taken humorously. The boys burst into laughter.

"Well, hell," I said, "Uncle Andrew is probably spooked out about being ordained and having so much lordly power that he needs something really strong to relieve some of the fear. I bet he's even more smashed than the others. And Jerry Hostetler; he thinks he's so high and mighty, that conniving stuttering son of a bitch. I bet he's enjoying my whiskey also. I hope they're all having a good time, those two-faced Preachers. They're nothing but hypocrites," I shouted slamming my fist against the wall. "They come together, drinking and stealing and just having a good time, yet if they catch us doing it, we get the crap whipped out of us." My heart was racing. I was furious.

"The whiskey and cigarettes cost me money," I said. "I'm going out there. They're going to have to pay me back."

"Hey, Christy, you stole that money, didn't you?" Petie said. Knowing he was right, we burst into laughter. However, I was determined to unmask the culprit who broke into my buggy and stole my whiskey, cigarettes and radio. The incident would not end here! I had to find the guilty man and settle the score.

After some consideration I eliminated Uncle Andrew concluding that old Preacher Hostetler with his 16 inch slick beard and sly glance had broken into my buggy. I made up my mind he would pay for his wrong doing, and I would make sure he did.

The following Sunday, Cousin Ruben, Wilmer, Petie and I walked over to Preacher Hostetler's horse. The animal was tied to the hay manger eating his oats. I grabbed a buggy whip.

"Wilmer," I said, excited about my avenging deed, "get another whip."

I flicked my whip twice in preparation then lifted my arm and came down hard on his back. The swish of the leather flying through the air was exhilarating. The horse neighed as the whip swatted his flesh and although I did not draw blood, several red welts began to appear under his hair. The painful whack of the leather slamming down on his back terrified him. Eager to get away, he lunged back. The rope snapped in half, freeing him from the hay manger. He took off, ran down the road and headed towards his home.

"Good," I said to the boys, "now that son of a bitch can just go out and look for his horse after Church."

I chuckled to myself, proud of my deed and feeling vindicated. If I could not whip the doer of an evil deed who had caused me injury, I'd just beat his animal. It was satisfying enough! It was the Amish way!

The next Church Sunday, Jerry's house was selected for service. After the last song, we went out to the barn. From the corner of my eye I spotted a kitten, scampering about. I leaned over and snatched the animal.

"This little son of a bitch is one of Jerry's kittens," I said to the boys standing nearby. "This cat has no right to be alive!"

"Kill the son of a gun, Christy," Petie shouted.

"You don't have to tell me what to do," I said. "This cat's already dead, only she doesn't know it."

I took the kitten over to the water tank and threw her in. The boys laughed. She sunk mid-way then reversed course and popped to the top. With my open hand I slapped her back down to the bottom, held her under for awhile and released my hand. The front of my shirt and my right sleeve were drenched. Once again she popped up, gasping for air and meowing. I again shoved her down to the floor of the tank but she came bouncing to the surface, still breathing.

"Get me a stick," I said, "This cat is tough."

One of the boys raced over with a long piece of wood. Snatching it from his hand, I hit the cat several times. She continued to resist, struggling to keep afloat until, weakened, she abandoned her fight for survival.

One Saturday afternoon, while doing my chores, Dad approached me in the barn.

"Christy," he said, clearing his throat. I had a feeling this was going to be a somber discussion; one that I would certainly not enjoy.

"You're nineteen and it's long past time you made a commitment to the Lord and the Amish Tradition. You're an adult and it's time to be baptized." Once again he cleared his throat.

"Christy," Dad said, "I strongly suggest you begin Sunday School preparation classes." While he spoke, I focused my gaze on his feet, avoiding eye contact. I remembered that just a year ago Dad had confronted me with Baptism and I had blatantly refused.

"I really don't want to make this commitment right now," I said raising my eyes to meet his for a brief second.

Dad said, "You've been confronted before and told you're old enough to assume spiritual responsibility. If something fatal should happen, you would face condemnation for denying the presence of the Lord. Do you understand? If you abandon God, if you refuse His presence in your life, there will be no hope of salvation for you. Is that clear Christy?"

"Well, Dad," I said, "I need to think about this a bit."

Dad said, "There is nothing to think about. You should not waste time considering whether or not to accept Jesus."

"It's not that, Dad. It's not about the Lord. I just don't think I want to put up with all the bull shit," I said boldly.

"What do you mean by that?" Dad asked. I knew he was irritated.

"All that crap in Church," I said. "Dad, you have a double standard. You favor the Elders. Edwin made bold remarks and you didn't punish him. However, if we say something not to your liking, even the dumbest little thing, we get beaten and humiliated."

Dad said, "As a young folk you are still involved in the learning process. The Elders have been there. They have gained wisdom through their experiences; therefore more credit is given to them." He paused to blow his nose.

"Christy," he continued, "I have taught you obedience. I have had many serious problems with your waywardness and refusal to keep the rules. If you insist on defying me and don't accept the Lord, there will be no hope and you will burn in hell."

"I'm not refusing the Lord. I'm rejecting the stupid Amish ways," I said, turning and walking away.

My daring outburst startled Dad. I felt queasy and upset. I knew I was being coerced into receiving Baptism. I was confused. Although Dad's tactic included a scheme to brain wash me into thinking I was sinning against the Lord, in my heart I didn't believe it. Even in the face of my confusion I was certain of one thing: I did not want to be baptized and become a member of the Amish Church! I was not ready to commit to something I knew I could not accept. It just did not feel right.

❋   ❋   ❋

Petie had become my partner and accomplice. I shared my drinking binges with him since I could no longer trust William to accompany me on my "outlaw" adventures. I knew William felt obliged to report to Dad every time I broke the rules and I thought it was wise not to provoke him.

After a round of serious hard drinking with Petie, we jumped on our courting buggies. These were much smaller than the standard buggies and did not accommodate more than two people.

"Diamond, let's go," I shouted, tapping him with the line. Quickly I yanked the right rein and he turned abruptly. The buggy was pulled in a complete circle, designing a doughnut in the gravel. Clouds of dust sprung around the wheels and bits of chipped stones splattered. I continued to repeat my command for Diamond to go and he obeyed, dragging and rotating the buggy, "cutting doughnuts."

After several spins the buggy capsized, breaking in the dash board. I was hurled ten feet down the road. The impact of my body hitting the gravel tore my pants and shirt sleeves. I scraped my arms and legs, drawing blood. My hat flew off my head, and landed under my butt. It was crushed by my weight, though it did little to buffer my fall. Scrambling to my feet, I turned and stomped on the hat, smashing it totally flat. I hated having to wear it all the time. Diamond came unhooked when the buggy overturned.

"Whoa, Diamond," I yelled. He halted instantly. It was amazing for a horse to obey a command as directly as he did. Observing the disaster I created, Petie jumped off his buggy and helped me set the buggy back on its wheels. It was sooty and scratched but not badly damaged. Afterwards we hitched Diamond up, dusted ourselves off and headed in opposite directions. I continued on my journey and just as Diamond reached the driveway, I passed out.

"Christy," Dad said, noticing I was lying flat on my back in the buggy, "What are you doing?"

The sound of his loud voice startled me, bringing me back to my senses. I opened my eyes and took a deep breath. I smelled a rancid odor and immediately realized I had puked all over the buggy.

"Christy," Dad continued, "did you hear what I said? I want to know what's going on. It's five o'clock in the morning."

"O, nothing," I said; "nothing's going on, Dad. I'm just drunk!"

"What, Christy!" he said, staring at me.

"Drunk," I said, "I'm drunk." Dad was irritated.

"Christy," he said, "this is a serious thing. How do you expect to be baptized when you don't obey the rules?"

"I don't know," I said, feeling dizzy. I closed my eyes, hoping to shut out the vision of Dad's irritated face spinning in front of me. I just wanted to get some sleep.

Dad turned and walked away, realizing he no longer had any influence on me. His power was drained. I had taken it, wrung it dry and shoved it down his throat.

I got to my feet, unhitched Diamond and stumbled upstairs to bed. Lying there reviewing last evenings' events I felt sorry for Dad. My conscience tormented me and I was unable to sleep. I tossed and thrashed about, listening to Mom cry. I knew she had been informed of my drinking. I felt sad for her. She was tightly locked in Dad's power, trapped under his control like all Old Order Amish women. It was her role in life. I hated the Amish Tradition and their senseless, hypocritical man-made rules.

No mention was made of my admitted drinking. The incident was dismissed even though talk of my impending Baptism continued.

The following Saturday evening, Dad and Uncle Andrew approached me.

"Christy," Dad said, "we would like you to start attending Sunday classes in preparation for your Baptism." Uncle Andrew nodded in agreement.

"Well," I said, shuffling my feet, "I really don't know. I haven't given it much thought yet."

"Christy," Uncle Andrew said, raising his eyebrows in a questioning way, "you do know that until you are baptized you cannot date a woman."

Although I respected Uncle Andrew, he irritated me with his

persistence. I felt pressured and reluctant to comply with their wishes.

"Yeah, Uncle Andrew," I said, "I know. But, uh, I don't know."

"Well, Christy," Uncle Andrew said, "we just want you to agree to start classes next Sunday. The classes will help you in your daily life. Everyone who has taken the classes has been enlightened and opened to the presence of the Lord."

"Well, OK," I said. "I'll do that."

"That's great, Christy," Uncle Andrew said, "you've made a wise decision."

"Yes, Christy," Dad said, "I'm very happy you have decided to proceed towards Baptism."

Dad was silent afterwards, realizing my decision to be baptized was not the result of his authority over me.

The preparation for Baptism would take six months but I knew I would do it my way and not in keeping with Dad's rules. As long as I did not get caught "breaking the rules," I would not be guilty of any wrong doing. The seed planted in Bowling Green, fertilized in Maywood, had sprouted in Kahoka. Now it was beginning to bud. However, it was still a bit too soon to see the nature of the bloom it would produce.

❋ ❋ ❋

Chapter 17

Dad and Uncle Andrew held firm to their convictions regarding my Baptism and, although I was neither enchanted nor at peace with the Amish Tradition, I agreed to follow the Sunday school classes which would qualify me to receive the sacrament and become a Church member. Even though I accepted their proposal, I continued to drink and engage in vindictive acts. I became confrontational, refusing the hypocritical behavior of the Amish community. I no longer relied on the teachings and opinions of my Dad to make responsible and independent decisions. My frustration grew as I searched within myself for the courage to battle the demons born of my Dad's inconsistent words and the double standards which triggered his confusing actions.

"Why does Dad have the power to condemn others?" I asked myself. "And why would I gain salvation only if I follow his rules?" I wanted answers.

Agreeing to be baptized, I attended Sunday school classes every other week for six months, together with Petie, Cousin Edna and two girls.

The Bishop was responsible for selecting the books that were used for Sunday school. I was not very interested in attending the classes and before they started I always drank a few whiskeys. Afterwards, I stuffed my mouth with several pieces of gum, to camouflage the evidence of wrong doing my foul breath betrayed.

Instead of the Bible, Dad and the Preachers taught Sunday school with Sammy Beiler's book written in 1857. Beiler was a highly decorated Old Order Amish Bishop from Lancaster County Pennsylvania who incorporated scriptural passages in his book to outline the basic principles for leading a good and virtuous life. After reading Beiler's work, I discovered it served exclusively as a brain washing tool to indoctrinate young folks.

The day finally arrived. The classes had ended and it was time to "come to know the Lord." Before the services started, those of us who were going to be baptized were instructed to sit on the bench directly in front of the Preachers. These seats were customarily reserved for the small boys.

Baptism in the Old Order Amish Tradition was a very solemn ritual. With three splashes of holy water over our heads we would meet the Lord and embrace Him in our lives. We would be considered true disciples of God and be expected to take on the responsibility of helping Him build and defend Church rules and the Amish Tradition.

I was not a very serious candidate for Baptism having consented against my better judgment. My demeanor was neither humble nor solemn. Rebellious and defiant, I tucked a pack of cigarettes into the tiny pocket on the inside of my dress coat. I wrapped a can of chewing tobacco in a handkerchief, and stuffed it in the pocket of my pants.

"I have to prove to myself one more time," I thought, "that the Bishop is not God."

Dad stood tall and preached his sermon, conveying his joy over the excitement of the young folks about to receive Baptism.

"Today is a special day. The parents of these young folks should be proud," the Bishop said glancing at me, Petie and the girls. "They have raised these young folks to be faithful followers of the tradition and today they will gloriously meet the Lord."

"He doesn't have a clue," I whispered to myself, shaking my head. "How can a man who holds himself up as a powerful Bishop and authority figure in the community be so blind to the truth? He's like Grandpa in a sense, although I'll admit he's more knowledgeable in his dealings with others. He's neither arrogant nor condescending in public, but interacts with others graciously and with a smile, be they Amish or 'English.'"

Dad was like a chameleon, able to switch personalities to fit the nature of the person with whom he was interacting. His power led him to be hypocritical, cruel and abusive at home yet gave him the ability to conceal his brutality in Church and among his flock. I understood how manipulative and conniving his power was and how wisely he used it to masquerade his failings to achieve his goals.

The Deacon summoned Mom from the kitchen and asked her to remove the girls' caps. She came forward and obeyed. Gently she pulled the ribbons, untying the bows, and lifted the caps. We were then invited to kneel in front of the bench. Mom stood nearby while the Deacon walked over to the water bowl and lifted it from the table. With his free hand he picked up a mug, walked over to Dad, and handed it to him.

Dad took the mug and approached us as we knelt.

"Christy," he said, "do you believe Jesus Christ is the Son of God?"

"Yes," I replied, "I believe Jesus Christ is the Son of God."

"Do you promise with the help of God to serve the Lord and the Amish Community, until death do you part?" The Bishop continued.

"Yes, I do," I said.

Dad moved from person to person until everyone pledged a belief in Jesus as the Son of God and a life-long commitment to serve the Amish Tradition. He then walked back to where I knelt and dipped the mug in the holy water bowl, filling it half way. With a turn of his wrist he poured water over my head three times, once after invoking each member of the Blessed Trinity.

"I baptize you in the name of the Father, the Son and the

Holy Ghost," he said. After he repeated the invocation in front of each young folk he returned back to me.

"Christy," he said, "in the name of the Lord arise!" I raised my head from its bowed position, extended my arm to meet his hand, and rose from my kneeling position. Dad kissed me on the lips. This ritual represented my first brother kiss as a Church member.

In the Old Order Amish Tradition it was customary, after receiving Baptism, to give a full kiss on the lips before Sunday service: It was a sign of peace.

When Dad reached the girls, he proceeded in the same manner, asking them to rise. Once they were on their feet, he stepped aside while Mom took their hand and kissed them on the lips. I always found this custom of men kissing men and women kissing women on the mouth somewhat humorous and often would chuckle as I observed the members kissing. I did not like kissing men on the lips and tried my best to resist, knowing it irritated Dad. I was now a baptized man, a full member of Church and responsible to the Lord for my thoughts and actions. I was expected to be faithful and loyal to the Tradition: I was Amish.

Although a baptized man, I continued to defy the rules. Along with the other young folks I opened three buttons on my shirt, and knotted a bright red handkerchief around my neck, western style. I noticed my sister Tina wore a heart shaped watch on her wrist; a gift from Rubin. When she flipped open the lid to check the time an "I love you" inscription greeted her.

"What's going on here?" I thought. "These two are cousins, are they planning to get married? Things are out of control, and Dad doesn't even know what's happening!"

Soon after, on a Sunday night after drinking and smoking, I returned home. Unsteady on my feet I staggered to the barn and removed Diamond's harness. My head was spinning and I felt a dull throbbing ache near my temples. My breathing was shallow and with every step I fought a losing battle to maintain my balance. I leaned against the side of the barn and slid down on my heels. I rested my head on my knees, hoping the dizziness would subside. The whiskey I drank earlier refluxed, causing me to gag. It left a sour taste in my mouth.

After several minutes I rose to my feet and stumbled towards the barn door. Nearing the bottle calf pen, I paused a moment to watch the calves settle themselves besides each other.

I opened the pen, and grabbed one of the calves by the hind legs, to avoid getting kicked in the groin. She squirmed nervously trying to break my hold. I dragged her out and shoved her into a corner of the horse stall.

I unbuttoned my pants and pulled the calf towards me, lunged forward and thrust my penis into her. She quivered several times then yielded to submission, powerless to my aggressive rage. Drunk beyond reason I shoved and lunged at her mercilessly, until I felt a staggering explosion in my groin. I looked down, realized what I had just done and felt sickened. Quickly I pulled up my pants, fastened the buttons, and kicked the calf back into the bottle pen.

I went into the house, stumbled up the stairs and threw myself on the bed. The nausea returned, stronger than before. I knew it was not caused by my overindulgence in alcohol but by my own wicked behavior. My depraved deed disgusted and horrified me.

"How could I have dishonored myself with such a vile action?" I thought sobbing. I knew I had too much whiskey, but there was no excuse for sinking so low. I had tumbled into the bottomless pit of a dark abyss. I had sinned against the Lord and against nature. There was nothing more evil I could possibly do. I loathed the shameful man I had become. Bawling and gasping for air I vowed I would never repeat that degenerate act again. This time, I honored my promise.

I was now one of God's people and my defiant actions and rebellious thoughts were serious sins. As a member of Church I knew I now walked in the direct path of the Lord. I was morally responsible for my deeds. I was obliged to control my actions if I did not want to face damnation.

I decided to calm down and try to release some of the anger

governing my life. The rage within my heart was overwhelming, pushing me into the path of an all consuming crusade. I was vindictive and it was agonizing. Making a decision was the first step; carrying it through was another!

One evening, after spending the day helping Jeff Murray put up hay, he accompanied me home in his truck. As we reached the barn, I noticed Dad was plowing with the six horse Belgian team. There seemed to be a commotion. I opened the door and jumped out. Instantly I spotted my buggy horse Diamond out in the field, hitched with the team. This was not a wise decision because buggy horses were neither sturdy nor heavy enough to pull the plough. I was enraged. No one was permitted to handle my buggy horse! The young folks took great pride in their horses. We dedicated time and energy, brushing their hair and combing their manes, keeping them sleek and lustrous. When they hit the daylight, the horses would glisten under the rays of the sun.

These animals were considered private property, and were as special to us as new cars were to the 'English.'

"Chris," Jeff Murray said, "I see your Dad's plowing the field today."

"Yeah," I said.

I wanted to confront Dad but realized I was too furious and would probably regret my actions later.

"William," I said as he walked out of the barn, "that son of a bitch has my horse hooked up."

"Yeah," William said, "I told him you'd be mad."

I said, "What did he say?"

William answered, "Dad's exact words were: "The way this horse has been running on Sundays I think he needs a little work out in the fields to tame him down."

"OK, that's enough," I said. "That's all I can take. Here I am trying my best to be good and respectful and that son of a bitch hooks my horse up because he thinks he's too fast. Well, William, I got a better explanation. I bet he's hooking Diamond up and working him to the bone to get even with me for coming home drunk one night. He's upset with himself and regrets keeping it a secret."

I turned and walked away. Dad was trying to settle the score with me. I was upset knowing Diamond would be injured, pulling with the big two thousand pound Belgian work horses. Once again I was bothered by the clear evidence of Dad's double standard. Seeking revenge by harming a man's animal was wrong for me. However, the Bishop was free to do as he pleased!

Later that evening, I gazed across the field and noticed Jeff Murray's residence was all illuminated. His lights glowed in the blackness of night, chasing the unknown shadows. They beckoned me in a silent way with a warmth and brightness that cut through the confusion and fear in my mind. It was a message of hope, a revelation and an invitation to begin my own journey. I knew what I had to do.

❋   ❋   ❋

Katie Girod was an elderly, handicapped, married woman with blue eyes and a strange knot engraved on her forehead which gave her a weird look. She had been ailing for some time and passed away.

I attended the funeral with cousins Rubin and Edna and my sister Tina. We drank quite a bit of whiskey during the five mile drive to the service. By the time we arrived I was drunk and unsteady on my feet.

"Rubin," I whispered, "I'm feeling a bit tired. I'm just going to sit here and rest my head on my lap. Wake me up when its time to kneel for the prayer."

Rubin, who had consumed about as much whiskey as I did, nodded his consent, although he also sat with his head lowered on folded arms. The room spun several times before I passed out.

I felt a sharp elbow burrow into my side and awakened with a start, realizing Rubin had nudged me. I knelt quickly for the prayer. After the service, we walked over to the casket to view Katie Girod's remains. I glanced down and noticed she seemed to move. Perhaps it was the drinking. Still saturated with whiskey, I had difficulty focusing my vision. However, the feeling was scary. My stomach plummeted. Death was not easy to digest.

I walked unsteadily. It was evident I had been drinking. Once back at the house, Dad approached me.

"Christy," he said, "have you been drinking?"

"Yes," I said. There was no way to deny my guilt and be credible. I was drunk!

"Christy," he said, irritated, "now you're dealing with the Lord. Do you realize I have to report this in Church?"

I felt his question and his comment were unworthy of either a response or rebuttal. My thoughts were centered exclusively on going upstairs to bed. I was not thinking clearly and had little if any interest to defend my point of view with Dad. It was just a waste of time anyway. I felt overpowered and knew I had to work through my disturbing thoughts.

The following Sunday in Church Dad announced that I, Wilmer Eicher and Cousin Rubin were guilty of attending Katie Girod's funeral drunk. Once confronted and accused, Wilmer and Rubin admitted their wrong doing. Confessing was a rare occurrence among young folk boys who customarily denied even in the light of undisputable evidence.

Dad was solemn; his pale, drawn face did not reflect a spirit at peace. It was damaging and disturbing for the Bishop to face his congregation and announce his son had been drinking.

After services that Sunday, a Special Meeting was held.

"Christy, Rubin and Wilmer," Dad said, "please rise and leave."

I obeyed his command, rose from the bench and walked out. Rubin and Wilmer followed in my footsteps. A strange silence came over me. I neither commented about my drinking and bad behavior nor joked about being cast out of Church.

A half hour later, the Preachers came to the door and motioned for us to return. We walked from the barn towards the house. I noticed Uncle Andrew was upset. His gaze was focused on his feet.

"We are ready to inform you about our discussion," he said addressing me, Rubin and Wilmer, "and the decision we have reached in Church this afternoon."

I felt a heavy weight press down on my chest. I swallowed hard, trying to clear the lump in my throat. I knew what was coming. I took my seat directly if front of the Preachers in the section reserved for the sinners. Dad came forward. His expression was taut; his eyes darkened by his own disappointment and embarrassment as well as the gravity of the issue he was obliged to judge.

I kept my head bowed and drew in a deep breath.

"You indulged in alcohol and you got drunk," Dad said, his voice quivering. "You have sinned against Church and directly against God."

He called each one of us by name.

"Christy," he said, "as a disciple of the Lord and in accordance with His word, I condemn you to hell!" He nervously cleared his throat. "The length of your sentence will be decided later. You may now leave the room and go home."

I stood and walked out, feeling humiliated and distraught. I was disgusted with myself and believed I was insignificant and unqualified to compete with the Amish Church members. Admitting my failure, though painful, relieved me of some of my anguish. I was no longer a part of the Amish Tradition. My thoughts turned to Dad. I imagined the intensity of his shame and the dishonor he felt, as a Bishop, obliged to condemn his own son. I had done wrong and he had no choice but to throw me out of Church.

I walked over to my buggy and climbed on.

"Diamond, let's go!" I said as he began to neigh softly. It seemed as if he understood my pain. I headed home alone, confused and troubled.

At supper that evening a chair was set for me in the back corner of the room. According to the Amish Tradition, a condemned man is not permitted any physical contact with the other Church members. Although my sister Tina was not yet baptized, she was old enough to know she was not allowed to touch me, directly offer me something, or accept anything from my hand.

Tina served me supper that evening. She placed the meal in front of me and carefully stepped away. Dad watched to be sure she was abiding by the rules. When she returned after supper to collect my plate, she approached me with her back turned towards Dad. I tried to slide the plate across the table, and aim for her hands to make it less complicated for her. However, she anticipated my action, reached over and took it directly from my hands, flashing me a bold look. Her courageous gaze assured me she was not afraid to defy Dad's rule.

I was sentenced to sleep in the trash room for six weeks as part of my punishment. This was a small, poorly ventilated area, used primarily to store household articles and discarded items. A stale, musty odor permeated the room, making it difficult to breathe. A dense layer of grey soot covered the shelves and gathered along the perimeter of the floor. Although the darkness helped minimize the mess, the dingy atmosphere was depressing.

A narrow cot was set up with a wrinkled, ill-fitted sheet. I was given a light cover and a hard, flat pillow that smelled of mildew. The mattress was pliable and lacked support. When I tossed and turned, which was quite often given the anguishing circumstances, the springs of the cot compressed under my weight, emitting an annoying squeak. To have a moment of quiet I forced myself to remain dead still, barely daring to breathe. I didn't have a choice. I was an outcast, a condemned man and not worthy to sleep in the same room with William or anyone else.

I spent sleepless hours contemplating the dreadful reality of the Amish Tradition and accepted as hopeless the idea of change. I rose every morning with a stiff and painful back. It was weak from all the lashings I received as a child and the unsteady cot served as a catalyst, aggravating my condition.

At the end of the six week period Wilmer, Rubin and I were placed on the sinner's bench in front of the Preachers. We were each called by name: I was first.

"Christy," the Bishop said, "have you had anything to drink during the past six weeks?"

"No," I lied.

Dad asked us to kneel down. We obeyed.

"Do you promise to keep the vows you made at you Baptism?" Dad asked.

We each responded, "Yes." Dad extended his hand.

"In the Lord's name, arise!" he said, taking our hands and lifting us to our feet, one by one. We renewed our Baptism vows and kissed him fully on the mouth, the kiss of peace I always despised.

After the peace kiss Dad delivered a short speech. His face was relaxed. His eyes seemed to have recuperated the glow which had dimmed after I was discharged from Church.

"It is with great joy we welcome every child of the Lord back to the fold," he said. "Sometimes a Shepherd loses one of his sheep. The loss causes much suffering and distress until the lamb is found and returned to the flock." Dad cleared his throat and continued, "Some time ago, three of our members lost their way and fell from the Lord's favor. Today they return, repentant and in peace with God. It is a joyful day: Our children have once again embraced the Lord; they have returned home."

I sat, without flinching, indifferent to the forgiveness granted and unaffected by the joy expressed in Dad's words. I was an outsider looking in. I moved with the flow, unguided by my thoughts and feelings. I was no longer interested in Church affairs. My decision had been made and even the Bishop's power would not be able to change my direction. My mind was made up: It was almost time.

❋   ❋   ❋

Chapter 18

In the midst of my confusion, anger and doubts one thing was certain: I was an outsider and an "outlaw." I blamed my falling away on Dad's conflicting ideas and rules as well as his ambiguous behavior.

My independent nature and free thinking prohibited me from tolerating Dad's ways. I questioned every aspect of Church and the Tradition. I wanted answers. I had to have my doubts turned into certainties and my unknowns brought into the light of truth. I was my own victim, a man trapped in a broken truth and shackled by a culture of violent abuse.

❈ ❈ ❈

Milford Burkholder, Mom and Dad's ninth child, was born in 1985. He was small and slim with captivating dark eyes and a charming smile. Milford was a spirited boy who seemed to share some of my characteristics. We had a special relationship and I always considered him my buddy despite the considerable age difference.

I remember the day Milford came home from school upset.

"Christy," he said, crying, "Teacher Beth whipped me with a strap today in front of everyone." Beth Yoder was an unmarried, unattractive nun who wore ugly wire-rimmed glasses we referred to as "birth control." She was considered odd and not well liked in the community.

"Why, Milford?" I said, already feeling his pain.

"'Cause I slipped and said a bad word, Christy," he said gazing down at his feet.

My mind flashed back to the severe beatings I received as a child. I felt the strap lash into my back. I felt the stinging wave of humiliation while the family watched the Bishop discipline me with his own brand of violence. I shuddered, recalling the agony of those moments. I felt sorry for Milford.

"Don't say anything to Dad," I told him. "Don't worry; I'll take care of it."

Milford looked up at me. His big dark eyes lit up.

"Christy," he said grinning, "I knew you would take care of it!"

I took a deep breath and felt a steady throbbing in my chest. My temper was erupting. I knew I could strangle Teacher Beth if she dared cross my path. I had witnessed Dad whip Milford. I heard the slash of his leather strap as it made contact with his back. I saw the helpless boy's agonized look. I relived my past: It sickened me.

I believed Teacher Beth had been unjust and crossed the line. If she was going to be cruel to my brother, I would reciprocate her evil deed. She would have to pay.

I told William that evening how brutally Teacher Beth had treated Milford and how I had reassured him I would handle the matter. Surprisingly he did not oppose my plan, but agreed to be my accomplice.

After chores were finished we pretended to go sparrow hunting. Once outside, we changed direction and headed for the school house.

"William, when we get inside we'll do something. We gotta get even with 'birth control' Yoder for what she did to Milford."

Doors were never locked in the Amish community, allowing

easy entry. We walked over to the school house and pulled open the door. It creaked like it had years earlier when I was a student. Nothing had changed.

I ran inside searching for something I could destroy. I was enraged, bubbling over with vindictive energy.

I shouted, "Let's find something we can rip to shreds. First of all we gotta find that damn strap Teacher Beth used to beat Milford, 'cause we're gonna burn it!"

Since it was early fall the wood stove had already been filled and lit during the day to heat up the school room. I walked over to it and noticed some of the coals were still simmering.

I went over to Teacher Beth's desk, yanked open the drawer and snatched her pencils, erasers and note papers.

William," I shouted, "throw these into the stove!"

I then ran over and grabbed her Geography, English and German books and hurled them into the quickly rising clouds of dark smoke. The charred aroma was exhilarating but not as thrilling as witnessing Teacher Beth's possessions smolder into cinders.

"Christy," William shouted from across the room, "I found it! I found the strap!" He held it up above his head. I looked quickly and noticed it was a three foot piece of worn brown leather.

"Burn it, William," I said.

William tossed it on top of the crackling coals. The leather sizzled as it melted. The fragrance of disarmament was arousing.

"Christy," he said, satisfied, "that's enough! I think we better go."

Although William was just as upset as I regarding the nasty lashing Milford received, he was able to control his anger, and certainly more willing than I.

"Just one more thing, William," I said, "and then we can get out of here. I'm not finished with ugly 'birth control' yet!"

I dropped my pants. "William," I said, grinning, "I have to poop and Teacher Beth will have to clean up the mess."

I walked over to the waste paper basket, spread my legs, saddled it and dropped a load.

I said, laughing, "Maybe I had too much shoofly pie at dinner!"

He chuckled. "Hurry, Christy," he said, "you're stinking up the place."

"I'm almost done," I said. "Hand me that book on old Teacher Beth's desk." William obeyed and handed me the book.

I ripped out a couple of pages, wiped my butt and tossed them into the waste paper basket.

"Man that was rough!" I said.

I kicked the basket under the desk, grabbed Teacher Beth's chair and positioned it nearby to assure myself she would not miss my aromatic surprise.

The following evening after the children had returned home, news of an act of vandalism at the school house spread through the community. Dad confronted me.

"Christy," he said, "do you know anything about the trouble over at the school house?" Without pausing for an answer, he continued, "somebody went there last evening and burned Teacher Yoder's books and some of her personal items."

"Yes, Dad," I said, "I did it and I'll do even more if she dares to give Milford another whipping."

Dad said, "What you did was seriously wrong. Milford was punished because he misbehaved. He deserved the whipping. I don't want you to do anything like that again. Do you hear me?" Dad took a long, slow, deep breath, not expecting a response. He didn't get one.

He continued, "Although Teacher Beth is not well liked you must realize she is still one of us here in the Amish Community. I don't want you to bother her. Do you hear me?"

I had no intention of obeying Dad's command. I knew that if Teacher Beth dared to whip Milford for whatever reason, I would not hesitate to settle the score. Revenge was my way of combating pain and humiliation. I believed in the law of retaliation: 'An eye for an eye and a tooth for a tooth.' It was written in the Bible! I was not sorry for my retributive actions and there would be no act of atonement. I was beyond penitence.

I was merely stalling for time. My mind was made up. I was leaving. However, the time was not yet right. I needed more information and a stronger dose of courage before I would be ready to turn my life around. Two buds had bloomed from the seed planted in Bowling Green. They were unusual, special: I questioned if the buds would perish before they had a chance to flower and mature. I needed additional answers and just a bit more patience.

✺   ✺   ✺

Chapter 19

Dad was no longer able to dominate me. This was the defining moment and he was faced with finding the solution to rectify the wrongs, knowing he was powerless and destined to fail. The conflict seemed unsettling and the consequences promised to be devastating. The Bishop was at the cross roads.

I was upset with myself, disturbed by the man I had forced myself to become. However, as a member of the Amish Church I was beginning to see I was not the lone sinner. The very deeds that disgusted and humiliated me were almost commonplace in the community.

One Saturday evening, Mose Mast, a tall, slender, intellectually limited man, came to the house to visit Dad. Several minutes later, Jacob Yoder and Amos Mast arrived. The men discussed outside for quite some time, exchanging news and opinions. This gathering of Elders signified something was brewing in the community. Either there was information leading to a young folk's dismissal from Church or they themselves were guilty of some evil deed. I knew there was trouble, but since Dad did not discuss it openly, I did not pose any questions.

The following day, after Sunday Service, a special meeting was called. Dad rose, cleared his throat and addressed the flock, holding his head rigid.

"It has come to my attention that there are a couple of 'brothers' among us who have fallen into sin," he said. "They have been guided by the Lord to come forward, confess their guilt and make amends." Dad paused and took a deep breath. "This involves Mose Mast, Jacob Yoder and Amos Mast."

Two of the men, Mose and Jacob, were married with children and Amos was single. Dad's words spelled trouble.

"Mose Mast," Dad said, "has indulged in sinful thoughts. He wishes to confess he willingly coveted his neighbor's wife while engaging in sex with his pregnant wife. His action was not guided by the purpose of procreation but the selfish attainment of personal gratification." Mose's sin was two-fold. He lusted after another woman, committing adultery in his heart, and he had needless sex with his wife, turning the act of procreation into a sin.

The Old Order Amish Tradition teaches that the sex act is evil if used for enjoyment. If a wife agreed to sex purely for pleasure she would be considered a whore and a grave sinner.

Dad announced that Jacob Yoder and Amos Mast, who were guilty of having sex with their horses, were ready to accept responsibility for their evil actions.

Amos, unlike Jacob and Mose, was single and childless. After the tearful admissions of wrong doings Dad asked them to leave and waited in silence until they departed.

After Dad announced their punishment to the waiting congregation the three men were called back to Church. The door creaked and slammed: They entered solemnly and knelt.

Dad reached out and beckoned for each man to rise to his feet. He stepped forward and gave them the kiss of peace, pardoning their sins.

I was unable to shake the disturbing thoughts of young folks and Elders engaging in sex with their horses. Although as a young boy I had tried it, repeating the degenerate act later on while drunk, I felt filthy and ashamed. I regretted my evil deed and knew I would never stoop so low again. Yet I was surprised to learn that this type of vile behavior was widespread in the Amish Community.

✹   ✹   ✹

In the Old Order Amish Tradition, Communion was held in the fall. It was a once a year event that involved breaking bread, sipping wine and a ritual that included washing feet. In a sense it was a reenactment of the Last Supper.

The service started at nine o'clock in the morning and ended around four in the afternoon with three Preachers and the Bishop recounting the story of Adam and Eve in the Garden of Eden. They traced the development of humanity from the beginning of life in the Old Testament, straight through the Crucifixion of Jesus in the New Testament. The events were recited by memory and only if the Preacher stumbled over a passage would he be handed the Bible. Another Preacher would follow the sermon and have the Bible opened to the page that corresponded to the event he was speaking about. When Dad delivered his sermon he neither faltered nor stumbled and did not have to be handed the Bible. There was no doubt the Bishop knew the Scriptures.

I was impressed with Dad's recount and marveled over the Biblical knowledge he demonstrated. I listened, eager for him to reach the Gospel stories. The Old Testament Books were boring and somewhat impractical to apply on a personal level. However, I loved the parables of Jesus and his disciples. They always fascinated me, imparted a lesson and, if taken seriously, could be a help in daily life.

The Crucifixion was a powerful episode. The details were emotionally compelling and I was always moved by the episode of Peter denying Christ three times.

As Dad told the story, I whispered the words ingrained in my memory:

"Then the maid seeing Peter…..said, 'This man also was with Jesus.' But he denied it saying, 'Woman, I don't know Him!'"

I thought to myself. "Even with a strong will and sincere commitment to do good, we often tumble into sinful ways. We try to conceal our fears and insecurities by denying the truth.

If Christ suffered and died on the cross to save humanity," I said to myself, "then why does Dad think he has the power to condemn to hell the 'English' or the Amish who break his rules?" This question, the Bishop would never answer!

Around three o'clock Dad summoned the Preachers to bring in the bread and wine.

Mom had baked the bread. It was kneaded with flour and water, thickly sliced and, unlike standard table bread, it was tasteless. Dad extended his hands and the Preacher put the bread in his palms. The members stood at attention, while the children and non members took their seats.

Dad gently lifted the bread and broke off a piece. Handing it to one of the members he said: "This is my flesh. Eat. This is a piece of my body." Dad repeated this invocation every time he handed someone a piece of bread.

The member accepted the bread, put it in his mouth, bowed his head and bent his knees twice before taking his seat. Bending the knees twice was a sign of respect and devotion and was also performed every time the name of God was mentioned during biblical readings, in accordance with the words written in Philippians: "That at the name of Jesus every knee should bow."

After the entire congregation had received, Dad recited a short prayer. At the end of the prayer he summoned one of the Preachers.

"Andrew," he said, "it is time for the wine." Andrew brought over a coffee mug and a bottle of Mogen David wine wrapped in a white cloth. Dad opened the bottle and filled the mug half way. The trickle of wine echoed in the stillness. I inhaled to enjoy the delicate scent permeating the room. It was an act of amnesty, offering momentary respite from the repulsive stench of sweat and foul breath so common in Church.

The members remained standing. Dad was followed by Andrew who carried the 'Mad Dog 20-20,' which was how we referred to the Mogen David wine. He refilled the mug when it emptied. Dad walked around offering the mug in the same manner in which he had distributed the bread.

"This is my blood: Drink!" The Bishop said to each person as he offered the wine.

When everyone was seated Dad placed the mug on the table. "Let us praise the Lord and raise our voices in song."

The diverse vocal tones and pitches mixed together created an unpleasant, dissonant tune.

During the singing, two Preachers quietly departed, went into the kitchen and returned, each carrying a large bowl. One was placed in the doorway of the kitchen and one in the living room, in front of the Preachers. A small two-seat bench was also placed in the entryway of the kitchen for the women, allowing the Elders and Preachers to see the action from the living room.

The Preacher set the stainless steel bowl down. From behind, another Preacher filled it mid way with water. The singing continued. Starting with the Elders in the living room, the men rose in pairs and washed each other's feet. They removed their shoes and socks and slid them under the bench. The odor was repugnant.

I watched an Elder roll up his pants, lift his leg, dunk his foot in the water, and quickly remove it. The second Elder, waiting at full attention, immediately bent over, grasped the foot and plunged it back into the water. He then washed it and reached behind for the towel that was set on the bench. Grabbing the towel, he covered the foot and dried if off with several brisk rubs. The procedure was repeated on the second foot. Afterwards the roles were reversed. When both men had completed the foot washing ritual they stood up, faced each other, shook hands and shared the full mouth kiss as a sign of peace.

The women and young folk men also carried out the ritual. They paired up, washed each other's feet and shared a handshake followed by a full mouth kiss.

That evening while my sister Tina and I rode home, I reached out and grabbed the bottle of whiskey I kept hidden under the dash.

Since Elma was spending most of her time with her boyfriend, Tina and I had become closer. We continued to drink while

Diamond paced. The alcohol seemed to appease my conscience, and appease my doubts of serious wrong doings.

Tina and I drank quite a bit of whiskey during the five mile ride home. The night air was crisp and we threw a blanket over our legs to keep from shivering.

"Do you want anymore to drink?" I asked Tina, offering her the bottle.

"No, Christy," she said giggling. I knew she was drunk!

Suddenly I felt Tina's hand brush against my leg, under the blanket. She caught me by surprise and I twitched. Grinning, she teasingly inched her way up to my groin. I felt a sharp tingle and took a big chug from the bottle. I was clumsy and agitated. The whiskey poured out too quickly and a few drops dripped down my chin. I immediately wiped them away with the sleeve of my coat.

I reached over and firmly grabbed one of Tina's breasts. She snatched the whiskey bottle from my free hand and gulped down a mouthful. Instantly, she reached for my penis and gave me a hard fast rub. My breathing quickened, my heart raced.

"This is wrong," I thought to myself. "But so many things are wrong."

Diamond slowed to a walk. Tina became more aggressive. She fumbled with the buttons on my pants, unbuttoned them, encircled her hand around my penis and massaged me vigorously until I climaxed.

"Wow, Tina," I said, trying to catch my breath. "That was wild."

"Yuck," she said, pulling her hand away and sliding it down the blanket to be rid of my semen. "Christy, that's a bit messy."

Confused, I emptied the whisky bottle down my throat and hurled it from the buggy. It hit the road and splattered, spraying the dirt with a shower of broken glass.

I knew I was guilty of wrong doing, even though Tina had provoked me by brushing against my thigh with her hand. I had goaded her further by caressing her breasts.

That evening, I passed a restless night. "This is incest!" I said to myself, appalled. My guilty conscience kept me wide-eyed. I was trapped on a dead end road. Here in Kahoka, there were no solutions, no answers and no more options. I walked as far as I could and discovered it was time to find another path.

The realization of how low I had fallen was devastating. I avoided Tina whenever possible and refrained from any eye contact. Just being in her presence disturbed me.

On Church Sundays, I rode alone to the services, asking William to accompany Tina. I invented excuses to seem credible then sat in the barn, drinking whiskey. I withdrew from everyone, tortured by my guilty feelings and thoughts of not belonging in the Amish Community. I became a loner, locked in the web of my own unsettled spirit. I knew there was only one way to triumph over my demons: I had to leave. I had to turn my back and walk away from my family, from Church and from the Community!

❈   ❈   ❈

Chapter 20

Power was not the answer, although my thirst for it motivated my life until I was able to see the demons hidden under the imaginary glory. I controlled my own thoughts and actions and my violent behavior patterns were evidence of my claim to independence. I wanted to disentangle myself from the suffocating hypocrisy. The knowledge that I would be shunned and considered dead by my family did little to complicate my decision. More than anything I wanted to repair my damaged self-esteem, heal my wounded pride and reacquire the gift of free will given to every individual at birth. My inability to cope with the dictates of the Amish Tradition frustrated me. My former fight for survival became a battle for life.

Dad allowed me to work for an 'English' man who lived about seven miles from my home. He was renovating his house and had gathered a team of Amish young folks to do the work. While working I met the 'English' man's son and liked him instantly. While working in his room, I noticed a pair of cowboy boots standing beside his bed.

"Those boots are cool," I thought.

When the 'English' man's son came into the room I mentioned that I thought his boots were cool.

"I'll give you twenty dollars for your boots," I said, pulling two ten dollar bills from my pocket.

"OK, Chris," he said. Puzzled, he extended his hand to take the bills.

"Are you allowed to wear cowboy boots?" he asked.

"No," I responded; "But I need a pair."

He shrugged his shoulders and put the twenty-dollars in his pocket.

"Now that I have my cowboy boots," I said to myself, "I'm prepared for my journey into the 'English' man's world. If I leave wearing my shabby Amish shoes, everyone will poke fun at me."

I was setting my plan in motion, piece by piece. It wouldn't be long now. I went home happy to have a least one pair of 'modern' boots.

Cousin Rubin and I had grown apart and I had begun to spend time with his brother Andy, a daring man with a boastful attitude who carried his head high when he walked. One day, Andy and I were helping our 'English' neighbor put up hay.

"Andy," I said while loading the wagon, "I'm going out for some beers this evening."

"How are you gonna do that?" Andy said.

"I asked one of the 'English' men to pick me up after dark," I said. "I told him to park at the end of the gravel road and I'd meet him there."

"I'd like to come along," Andy said. "Can you pick me up? I can get out of the house when my dad goes to bed."

"OK Andy," I said; "Don't be late."

I knew I had the entire night to drink and was certain my evil deed would not be discovered if I was home in time for early morning chores.

Everything went smoothly. I left the house quietly. The 'English' man waited for me at the designated spot and I arrived promptly. Andy was also on time and was waiting when we neared his house.

The 'English' man dropped us off in St Francisville and we headed to the Buck and Bull bar. When we entered, the room became silent. The bar was warm, smoky and smelled of whiskey. A faint sound of clinking glass accompanied animated voices and loud explosions of laughter.

Dressed in our Amish clothes, with our big black hats, Andy and I drew a lot of attention. We were certainly different; odd, but interesting in a mysterious way.

I had become friends with the owner of the Buck and Bull bar while on a previous turkey hunt. When he spotted me entering, he flashed me a wide grin and motioned for me to come over.

"Hey, what're you guys drinking," he shouted.

"We'll have a couple of beers," I responded.

All eyes focused on us as we walked closer to the bar.

"The drinks are on me," an 'English' man said, coming over to introduce himself.

"Give these guys two beers on me," he said to the bartender.

We discovered we did not have to pay for our drinks that evening. Andy and I were rather fascinating to the bar patrons who continued to buy us drinks in exchange for a few words about Amish life. They did not mock our guttural German accent but thought we were cool. For the first time in my life I felt at ease and connected to the 'English.'

"These people are not bad," I thought.

We chatted and spent a delightful evening enjoying the 'English' men's company. I felt a liking and an attraction to these congenial people whom Dad presented as evil individuals, condemned to hell because they were not living the Amish Tradition.

"Well," I said to myself, gulping down an icy beer, "I really don't care if the 'English' are condemned, 'cause I'm probably going to hell also."

When it was time to leave the bar, we were invited to return.

I felt a strong connection to the 'modern' world and knew I could easily bond with the 'English.' This was part of their way of life; a lifestyle that did not result in punishment, humiliation or shame for enjoying a few beers.

"There is no commandment that says: Thou shalt not drink or smoke!" I thought to myself; "And the Lord never said we must always wear a big flat brimmed hat, high buttoned shirt and baggy black pants or we'll go to hell."

I liked the feeling of freedom and couldn't accept the idea that the Lord gave free will and punished those who used it to drink a beer, smoke a cigarette or drive a car. It made no sense at all.

It was late when I returned home. Even nature was asleep. I removed my cowboy boots and tip-toed up the stairs, trying to hit the right spots to avoid the squeaks and creaks until I was safe in my room.

Andy was less fortunate. He was too drunk to climb the tree that would allow him entry into his room without waking Uncle Edwin. He went inside and was caught by his dad the moment he stepped over the threshold.

Uncle Edwin beat Andy severely with a long leather strap until he admitted his wrong doing. The following morning he came to the house to visit with Dad, driving his horse and buggy at an abnormally accelerated pace. Dad met him at the door and judging from his smug attitude and smart aleck sneer I assumed Uncle Edwin's news was serious. The two men conversed for about twenty minutes. Afterwards I received confirmation that my feelings of impending trouble were correct.

Dad approached me as soon as Uncle Edwin jumped on his buggy and rode away.

"Christy," he said, "were you out until late last evening?"

"No, Dad," I lied. "Well, Christy," Dad said, "Edwin told me Andy told him everything that happened last evening at the Buck and Bull."

I looked at Dad. I knew it was senseless to lie. One fib leads to another and I was tired of it all; the bogus excuses, the indignant cover-ups and the spiteful denials. I no longer wanted to live entangled in a web of broken truth.

"Yeah, Dad," I said, "I was out late last night and came home drunk." I stood tall and took a deep breath. I said, "Eventually you're going to kick me out of Church. Why wait any longer? I really don't care any more."

I could see Dad was anxious. Tiny beads of sweat formed

along his creased forehead. His eyes met mine briefly before he blinked and pulled away. Nervously he readjusted his gaze to the floor.

Dad said, "You've got a drinking problem."

"No, Dad," I said boldly. "I drink to spite the Church!"

"Why do you want to spite the Church?" he said.

"Well, Dad," I said, "you just don't understand. I never agreed with your rules. You preach in Church but don't follow your own set of laws. The Elders are forgiven for telling lies, yet if I get caught fibbing I'm beaten. The hypocrisy makes no sense. I only consented to be baptized so I could date a woman."

"I don't believe that, Christy," Dad said taking a deep breath; "That's just wild talk! I poured water over your head three times; I baptized you myself. You're an Amish member of Church. You made a commitment to Church. You promised the Lord to defend the Amish Tradition and no other until death do you part!" he said, visibly agitated.

My fear of eternal damnation in the fires of hell was a reality that kept me from responding. I knew I was headed in that direction and I was fully aware that Dad did not have the power to change the situation.

"Christy," Dad said, responding to my silence, "can we do something for you?"

"No, Dad," I said. "There's nothing you can do."

"What do you mean, Christy?" he said. I noticed he had a strange look in his eyes.

"Dad," I said, "I'm just sick and tired of everything. I was never really convinced about Church and Baptism and I'd just rather forget it all."

Dad gazed at me with a mixture of confusion and defeat.

"Christy," he said, softening his tone, "did I do something wrong to warrant this refusal of Church and the Tradition?"

"No, Dad," I said.

I did not have the heart to tell him the whole truth.

Revenge was no longer my quest and I was certain that revealing the painful truth would not give me any satisfaction.

My intention was focused exclusively on leaving the Amish Tradition. I neither harbored a loathing for Dad nor a desire to cause him any more anguish and pain.

Dad was a defeated man: The Bishop's spirit was crushed! All his power as the supreme authority in the community could not save him from the dishonor and humiliation he suffered by my repeated misdeeds and refusal to embrace the Tradition.

Discussing with Dad would have only provoked a nasty confrontation and since I was an 'outlaw' and not in favorable standing with Church, my word was not considered reliable. Even as a member I was looked upon as an unfavorable witness to truth. The Bishop's son was a man with no credibility.

Dad walked over to his rocking chair and took a seat. I stood watching him rock, listening to the squeaks as he moved forward and backward.

"Maybe he finds the rhythmic movement calming," I said to myself.

I fidgeted with the buttons on my shirt. There was nothing more I could say. I made my point.

"Christy," Dad said, "you know I have little choice but to inform Church about what is happening."

"That's OK, Dad," I said shrugging my shoulders. "It's your job."

He looked at me oddly. I realized he had faced the truth; he accepted the fact I did not care. Our glances met for a brief silent moment before I turned around and went upstairs. I knew in my heart Dad would never believe me if I told him he was at fault for the misbehavior of the Kahoka young folks. It was useless to even try.

The following Sunday I was kicked out of Church.

The Bishop was obliged to condemn his eldest son to hell! There could be no greater tragedy in the Amish Tradition.

I rose, aware that all eyes were fixed on me, stood tall and walked out. I knew that was the last time I would leave Church: The bud had grown tall on the stem, but the flower hung limply. Its petals failed to bloom.

I hitched up Diamond and rode home alone. Agitated and disgusted, I reached under the dash for a bottle of whiskey I had hidden. I grabbed it and opened the cap, dropping it as I rushed to swallow a big mouthful. I continued to drink as Diamond paced. When I arrived home, I ran upstairs to my room, clutching the bottle.

William and Tina walked into the house while I was drinking. At the sound of their voices I lowered the bottle and swung it behind my back.

"Christy," William said stepping into the bedroom, "I'm going over to Uncle Andrew's."

"OK, William," I said, "I'll see you later."

Tina went into her room. I quickly took a few more gulps of whiskey. Suddenly I heard the door to my room creak and noticed Tina standing in the entryway.

"Do you want a shot of whiskey?" I said, shoving the bottle in her face.

"OK, Christy," she said grabbing the whiskey.

We enjoyed a few laughs while we drank and discussed the day's events.

"Christy," Tina said, "I'm a bit tired. I'm going to my room to lie down for awhile."

After she left I reflected on my decision to leave Kahoka that evening. The time had come. I was kicked out of Church and had no intention of making amends. I thought about discussing my plan with Tina. She was a daring young woman who was not afraid to drink with me even though Dad had expelled me from Church. She defied the rule that forbade any contact with a condemned person and accepted the bottle from my hand. Tina didn't seem to care.

I stood up and walked into Tina's room, still holding the bottle of whiskey. She was lying on the bed.

"Christy," she said flashing me an alluring look, "Cousin Mose and I made out several times and we never got caught."

I was seated alongside the bed, fighting the urge to ask her to leave the Amish Community with me. I sat and continued to drink. My thoughts were an agonizing medley. Confused and tormented, I decided nothing mattered anymore. I was cast out of Church. I was an 'outlaw,' condemned to hell.

"Hey, Tina," I said, "are you feeling naughty?"

"Well, Christy," she said giggling, "I'm so drunk I could do anything!"

"O, really," I said. Her seductive manner aroused me. I rose to my feet, jumped on the bed and cupped her breasts in my hands, fondling them with firm rhythmic movements. Without pausing to unbutton my pants she grabbed my penis and gave me several hard squeezes. I pulled away, unfastened my pants, took them off and climbed back on the bed. I was breathless and compelled by a desire too strong to resist.

I lifted her dress and arched over her, excited. She reached up and pulled me down on top of her. The site of her half naked body startled me back to reality. Shocked, I jumped up and slipped on my pants, fumbling with the buttons.

"Tina wants to have sex with me," I said to myself, running back to my room, upset and confused about what had just occurred.

I cussed using every bad word I learned, trying to stomp on my guilt-ridden conscience. I knew drinking and smoking were wrong, but incest was an appalling and scornful sin.

I took a deep breath and returned to Tina's room to see if she was OK. She was covered and passed out on the bed. I took advantage of her unconscious state and quietly snuck over to her piggy bank. Quickly I emptied the change into my pocket. The coins jingled when I turned to leave. I put my hand over my pocket to muffle the sound.

Back in my room I gathered the nickels and dimes William and I had earned shooting rats in Maywood. I remembered that every time we showed Dad a dead rat he would give us a nickel to put in a jar. It all seemed so long ago.

I counted the change I had accumulated. It amounted to seven dollars and twenty-five cents. I put the coins in a jar and shoved it in one of my cowboy boots, hidden in the closet.

I despised myself; my life was a whirl of pain, misery and anguish. I felt filthy and disgusting. My behavior appalled me and I looked for excuses to isolate myself from the family and from Tina. I avoided Dad, unwilling to accept confrontations. I felt alone even before my actual departure.

I walked around in a daze no longer tending to my chores and refusing to help milk the cows. My body was present but I was no longer a part of the community. It was easier to deal with physical hurts than the agony of an emotional pain that never subsided. I had to do something.

One evening after work I parked my buggy in front of the Buck and Bull bar and drank until I was intoxicated. I no longer feared punishment and didn't care who saw me. That evening I returned home around ten o'clock. I swung open the door and walked in. Dad looked up from his book when he heard the door squeak.

"Christy," Dad said continuing to rock in his chair, "did you have to work late this evening?"

"No," I said making my way over to the stairs. "I didn't have to work late."

I sensed that Dad was upset by my bad behavior.

"Does Dad know what's going on here?" I asked myself. "Will he finally realize what's happening? Will he ever see the whole truth?"

I answered my own questions.

"Dad will never change. He's the Bishop," I said accepting reality. "It's time I let go of this vendetta to dishonor and shame him. He tried his best to help me but failed."

It pained me to see Dad sitting in his rocking chair. His face was creased and tense, his complexion ashen. The image of this defeated man whose spirit had been so badly shattered disturbed me.

Dad was bullheaded and always stood up for his convictions. I had been shamefully disrespectful towards him and to bear witness to his humiliating downfall was agonizing. This was the man I admired and wanted to be like during my boyhood years in

Maywood. This was the man I looked up to and respected: He was my hero! Today, however, as a young man, I looked at him with pity. For the first time in his life, the Bishop was locked in silence. Confused and overpowered, he was unable to save his own son.

My thoughts seemed to circulate more freely. In the darkness and amid the chaos I accepted the bare truth: I loved Dad! It was a feeling trapped within. He would never know because in the Amish Tradition words of love were never spoken.

I had tried to fight my feelings, wanting to hate him so desperately. All the time and energy I dedicated to the lies and avenging deeds had helped me regain my misplaced dignity; even if just in the early years.

Accepting my own reality and finalizing my decision to leave, I vowed I would take with me and treasure the qualities I respected and shared with my Dad: His courage to stand up for his ideals and his loyalty towards his beliefs.

I made a promise to be honest and sincere with myself and others and never assume the role of God in judging or condemning another human being. I knew in my heart, once free, I would walk forward, growing and learning from my painful experiences. I knew I would strive to become a better man and dedicate my life to encouraging others to stand up for their rights and overcome their demons.

❋   ❋   ❋

Chapter 21

I had fallen so low I hardly recognized myself. After much deliberations and painful conflicts to overcome, I was ready to face the truth.

While everyone was busy milking the cows, I went into the buggy shed and found a heavy fifteen foot rope. I picked it up, and quickly left. I went to the house and took it upstairs. Once in my room I unraveled the rope, tied five knots, each separated by three feet, and hid it in my closet. I wrapped it in a heavy blanket and pushed it behind my cowboy boots.

I contemplated my escape minute by minute to be certain I had covered all the details. However, leaving the community meant severing all ties with my family. I'd be totally on my own without support once I stepped into the 'modern' world. My thoughts were overpowering. I fought my insecurities, losing myself in my own doubts. I knew what I was running away from but did not have the slightest idea what I was running towards.

The following day everything was ready for my escape. It was Friday and I had asked an 'English' man for whom I worked to wait for me near the gravel road. He was agreeable to my request.

During milking, I approached Mom.

"Mom," I said, "I'm going into the house for a minute." I knew the milking would take a bit more time. I walked upstairs feeling anxious. I could feel my strong steady heartbeats and a sinking feeling in the pit of my stomach.

I threw myself on the bed allowing the turmoil to paralyze me for a brief moment. I gazed around the room, snapping mental pictures with my eyes.

The house seemed so quiet. I got up from the bed and walked into Milford's room. I was overcome with emotion. I remembered his words to me whenever he was not feeling well.

"Christy," he'd say, "when I'm all alone in my room, I'm scared of the dark and can't sleep."

I would try to calm him down, reassure him that everything was OK and tell him to be brave. He always followed my advice. Many times when his fears became too difficult to deal with he would ask me if he could come into my room and stay awhile with me and William. I stood looking down at his little bed and regretted not allowing him to sleep more often with me. I knew I would never have the opportunity again and realized the price I would pay for my freedom would include losing Milford.

Milford seemed to be following in my footsteps with his curious, questioning mind and penchant for independent thinking. I prayed he would not have to struggle through the turmoil and agony I did while growing up.

"Who will defend Milford?" I asked myself.

I regretted not spending more time with him. But regrets should be prevented not encouraged. They serve only to increase anxiety and produce no solutions.

With a heavy heart I trudged back to my room. I opened the closet, pushed the blanket aside and grabbed the rope I had prepared. Walking over to the window I pushed it over the ledge. I fastened the end I was holding to the bed post, securing it with several large knots. To test the strength of my knots I gave the rope three hard tugs. My pulse raced. I snatched my cowboy boots and slid into them not daring to breathe. Then I reached for the coin jar and emptied the seven dollars and twenty five cents in my pocket. It was the moment of truth: I was leaving the Amish Tradition.

I hesitated, allowing my emotions to interrupt my plan. Memories of my own boyhood returned. I saw familiar faces, smiles, tears, grimaces, stern, scolding looks and intimidating glances. I felt the pain and humiliation of double hand slaps, leather strap whippings and the agony of wood sticks crashing down on my back. My escape this evening would close the door forever on everyone and everything that was part of my life until today. Despite the emotional pain of leaving my family, my mind was made up: I was moving towards the freedom I craved. I knew there would be a stiff price to pay.

I looked around the room once more, took a deep breath and climbed out the window. Entwining my legs around the rope, I slid down, hand over hand, until my feet touched the ground.

I darted down the gravel road and noticed Buster was by my side. He kept up with my pace and wagged his tail, excited about a new adventure: Maybe even coon hunting.

I paused a moment and Buster stopped alongside me. His eyes were bright in the darkness. I sat down and he edged closer. His wagging tail swatted the side of my leg. His breath was heavy and I recognized his panting as a sign he was ready for an exciting escapade.

"Buster," I said gently patting him on the head, "I'm leaving. You'll have to stay here because I don't know where I'm going."

Buster's ears flattened and his tail froze. He lay down beside me. His moist nose rubbed against my leg. I think he understood something unpleasant was happening. He winced and looked up at me with sad, almost teary eyes.

"Buster," I said petting his back, "I told Milford to be sure no one beats or mistreats you and I know he'll protect you." I was sobbing.

Without looking back, I continued my journey down the path of no return.

Christy, the Amish young folk, was dead. A new man was born that evening; a free man.

I reached the end of the road and spotted the 'English' man sitting in his vehicle waiting for me.

"Hey, Chris," he said, "Are you OK?"

"Yeah," I said, "I'm fine."

"Are you in any trouble?" he said looking me over. He did not know he was a factor in my escape plan and thought I was just sneaking out for a night of fun.

"I need to go down to the bar," I said.

"That's a surprise," he said grinning.

I did not tell him about my decision to leave the Amish Community. It was a solitary choice and a single-handed action.

Once in the bar, I received a lot of attention and questions from everyone. Although I no longer considered myself Amish, I still looked like one.

Even though I was questioned because of my unconventional appearance, I was neither ridiculed for my unique manner of speaking nor poked fun at for my dowdy clothes. Instead, the 'English' patrons, fascinated by my diversity, offered me drinks.

"How different this world is from the Amish Community," I thought to myself. Taking a deep breath I stepped forward and joined them in their quest for fun, enjoying the beers they generously offered.

Around one thirty in the morning, after the bar closed one of the men who paid for my beers approached me. He was unlike the others, seemed a bit eccentric and had an odd way of tucking his pants into his boots. Although there was no definable dress code in the bar, somehow he managed to present a strange image. His peculiar look drew attention.

"Where are you living?" he said, wiping the sweat off his forehead with his shirt sleeve.

"Well," I said, tilting myself back on the heels of my cowboy boots. "at the moment I'm kind of just having some fun and not staying in any one place."

"Why don't you come home with me?" he said. "I don't live far from here."

"I have a place to stay!" I thought to myself, relieved.

"OK," I said. "That sounds great!"

We left together and on the way home he pulled into a liquor store, ran inside and returned carrying a twelve pack of beer.

After a twenty minute ride and some good hearty laughs we reached his house.

"Chris, do you smoke?" he said, clearing his throat.

"Yeah," I said stepping into his living room.

"Good, Chris," he said, "'cause I got some real good stuff you'll enjoy."

He reached into his pocket and pulled out a small package wrapped in cellophane.

"That tobacco looks a bit weird," I said to myself.

He took the green stuff and rolled it up in the old fashioned way.

"Wow," I thought to myself, "this guy's pretty cool."

He turned on the TV, lit the cigarette, took two puffs and handed it to me. I leaned forward, grabbed it and brought it straight to my mouth.

"Pass me the cigarette, Chris," he said after I had taken several drags.

"This is weird," I thought to myself, "why can't he just roll two instead of sharing one?"

After taking several more puffs my head started to spin and I noticed the images on the TV screen, blurred. I felt dizzy and rubbed my eyes, believing it would subside.

"Is that getting to you, Chris?" the 'English' man said chuckling.

"What is this?" I said raising my hand with the cigarette fixed between my fingers. "It's pretty strong stuff and doesn't smell much like the tobacco I've smoked."

"That's weed, Chris," he said laughing.

"Weed? What kind of weed?" I asked puzzled.

"Marijuana! Chris, haven't you heard about Marijuana?" he said chuckling.

"O, wow," I thought to myself, "I'm doing drugs!" My heart was racing. "I could get caught and go to prison!" I thought, holding my breath. "This is serious stuff. People go to jail for doing drugs!"

"I don't feel very well," I said to the 'English' man, handing him the weed. "I think I'll just sit here and watch TV."

I was fascinated by the sounds and images portrayed on the TV. Mesmerized, I watched a Western movie, unable to take my eyes off the animated figures coming to life in front of me.

I continued to glare at the TV, turning my head every time one of the characters focused his gaze on me. The direct eye contact disturbed me. I knew the actor was not a real person, yet he was talking to me and looking at me.

I remembered Dad's words about the evil nature of the 'English' man's TV. He told me it was a means to sin and condemnation.

At dawn my eyes were bleary from the overindulgence in beer, the puffs of weed and the endless hours of TV.

"I think we'd better get some sleep," the 'English' man said, rising to turn off the TV.

He showed me into a bedroom. "You can sleep here," he said pointing to a disheveled bed. I noticed the room had a musty odor. It wasn't very inviting but I did not have a better option.

After the 'English' man departed, I walked over to the door, and quickly locked it. Although this man was kind to offer me a place to stay, he certainly did not inspire confidence. He did drugs and I was guarded and apprehensive.

I undressed, emptying the change from my pockets, and threw my pants on the side of the bed. I slid my seven dollars and twenty-five cents under the pillow. It was all I had and I was sure I would need it for food. Although the 'English' man was nice to me, he looked shifty and I didn't trust him.

"He might steal my money," I said to myself.

I climbed into bed and reviewed in my mind the past day's events, feeling a bit lonely for my family. "They must know by now," I thought. However, the excitement of my escape and the new adventures waiting to be experienced overwhelmed me.

Later that morning I awakened somewhat groggy. I jumped

out of bed, reached for my pants and hurriedly dressed myself. Walking to the head of the bed I lifted the pillow, gathered my coins and put them in my pocket.

When I went into the living room, the 'English' man was standing in front of the TV.

"Chris," he said, "where do you want to go?"

"Well," I said, "I'd like to return to the bar."

"Sure, we can do that," he said, grinning, "but it's only ten o'clock in the morning."

He drove me back to the bar. Sitting beside him I smelled a foul odor.

"He's not Amish but he stinks just as badly as they do," I said to myself. I wondered if he took a bath only on Saturday nights like the Amish and if so why, since he was free to wash up whenever he wanted. No one forced him to walk around stinking of sweat and bad breath.

"Well, Chris," he said when we reached the bar, "I guess I'll see you here tonight."

"OK," I said turning to open the door. "Thanks for the ride and for everything."

"You're welcome, Chris," he said.

I went into the bar and was happy to see the bar owner busy at work, checking the books. He was a recognizable face in a strange new world and the familiarity was comforting.

"Chris," the bar owner said, looking up from his books, "do you know that guy who just dropped you off?"

"No," I said.

"No! Then what are you doing with him?" he said. "Where are you coming from at this time of day?"

"I met him here last evening and he invited me to spend the night at his house," I said.

"He's a bit strange, isn't he?" the bar owner said.

"Yeah, actually he acted a bit weird," I said. "Anyway I probably won't stay at his house again."

"Well, where will you stay, Chris?" he asked.

"Nowhere," I said.

"What do you mean nowhere?" he said.

"Well, uh, I left home," I said.

"What?" he said, raising his voice, "You ran away from home!"

"Yeah, I guess," I said, looking down at my feet.

Immediately he called out to his wife who was in the kitchen preparing the day's menu.

"Emily," he shouted, "You won't believe it; this boy ran away from the Amish!"

Emily came out quickly and I noticed her white apron had several food stains down the front.

"Really! You did?" she said, staring at me wide-eyed. "Why did you run away?"

"I don't want to be Amish," I answered. "I'm kind of hungry," I said, changing the subject.

"Well, what would you like?" she asked.

"I don't really know," I said, "whatever you have."

"How about some bacon, eggs and toast?" she said.

"Sure, that sounds great," I said.

I stared at the TV while she prepared my breakfast. The aroma of the bacon and eggs frying in melted butter was tantalizing and the animated images talking and moving on the TV captivated my attention.

When Emily served me I offered to pay for the meal, however both she and her husband refused my money. I was surprised by their generosity.

After breakfast the bar owner approached me.

"What are you going to do now?" he said.

"I'm not going to be Amish anymore!" I responded.

"Well, Chris," he said, "in that case you better get some new clothes."

"Well, I don't have any money," I said, staring down at my big, wide pant legs.

"Hey," he said, "we have some clothes you can wear."

"O, no," I said. "That's OK. These clothes are fine."

"Not that Amish hat," he said laughing and pointing to my black felt hat; "You'd better get rid of that!"

"OK," I said walking out. "I'll be back later."

The bar owner told me there would be another party that evening and I was welcome to attend.

I returned to the bar that evening, eager to have some fun and to learn more about the 'English' man's way of life. I looked around the room and spotted Jim, an 'English' man who knew my Dad quite well. Our glances met and he waved.

"Hey," Jim said walking over to me; "What are you doing here?"

"I'm here to listen to the band," I said.

"Where are your folks?" Jim asked.

"I don't know," I said.

"What do you mean you don't know?" he asked puzzled.

"Well," I said taking a deep breath, "I left home. I'm no longer Amish."

"Judging from the way you're dressed," Jim said chuckling, "with those big baggy pants and that hat, it certainly doesn't seem like you're no longer Amish."

"I left the Amish," I said. "I don't have any money to buy clothes."

"Come on, get in the truck," he said. "We'll fix that problem."

We took a short drive to Jim's house.

"This is going to be your night out," Jim said. "You'll look real cool once you get rid of those pants and shirt and put on a different hat. Would you like something to drink?" Jim asked.

"Yeah," I said, "some milk would be fine."

Jim went into the kitchen. When he returned he was carrying a glass of milk.

"Here, Chris," he said, "It's nice and cold."

I quickly took a long drink.

"What's wrong, Chris?" Jim said, catching my grimacing reaction to the cold milk.

"O, nothing," I said feeling guilty and lowering my eyes.
"Looking at your face it seems like something tastes bad." Jim said. "Is the milk sour?"
"Well, no," I said. "It tastes like there's water in it."
Jim took a few steps towards me and playfully slapped me on the back.
"Chris," he said laughing, "you're just used to that rich, fatty dairy milk."
I was confused and didn't quite understand what he meant. As far as I was concerned the milk tasted like watered down crap.
Jim said, "Don't worry, the milk's fine. It's just pasteurized."
I gulped it down, holding my breath to deaden my taste buds. The watery milk was cold and burned my teeth. I noted it was more transparent, lighter in texture and lacked the rich hearty flavor of the milk I grew up on.
After my first 'modern' milk experience, Jim came forward handing me a pair of Levi's. They looked cool and fit perfectly.
Jim excused himself and went into another room, returning several minutes later with a colorfully patterned western shirt, a white cowboy hat, a smooth leather belt with a big silver buckle and a pair of highly polished boots. I was speechless. The western clothes gave me a sense of security about my decision and encouragement to proceed along this new and unknown path.
Gazing at me all dressed up Jim said, "Where are you going? You need a place to stay?"
"Well," I said, "right now I really don't know. I'm sure I'll find someone who will offer me a place."
"Chris," Jim said, "I've got a camper in the back yard that I use for camping trips. It's empty right now and you're welcome to stay there as long as you wish."
"Thanks," I said looking at him surprised. I was unable to express more than one word of gratitude.
I was taken aback by his kind offer. The generosity and warmth he demonstrated were amazing. I knew I would never forget him.
That evening, Jim and I went back to the bar for a night of

dancing and drinking. I had never danced before and keeping pace with the band's rhythmic sounds looked challenging.

"How can they move together without stepping all over each others feet?" I thought to myself, chuckling as I watched a couple gracefully glide on the dance floor. I followed their steps with my eyes, amazed by the performance.

That evening I had been introduced to many people and shook endless hands, becoming the center of attention. The 'English' were gracious and generous with their comments, complimenting me on how nice I looked in my 'modern' clothes. I felt confident and good about myself. No one had ever spoken about my appearance or praised me for anything. It was a new feeling and I enjoyed the consideration and approval of others.

"Hey, you're a good looking Amish," one of the ladies said. "Would you like to dance?"

"No," I said, nervously, "I don't think so."

"O, he just needs a few more beers," Jim said laughing.

Jim ordered another round and, afterwards, I succumbed to the lady's implorations and agreed to dance with her.

She tried to teach me a few steps but, being totally awkward and unaccustomed to following music, I repeatedly tripped over my feet, squashing her toes under the weight of my heavy boots. Music and dancing were not permitted in the Old Order Amish Tradition. It was the 'English' man's way and it was evil.

The bar became silent, the dance floor cleared and all eyes focused on the guest of honor: The ex-Amish boy who was taking his first steps on the dance floor.

I continued to trip and stomp on the lady's toes. It was obvious I was giving a clumsy performance. Jim spoke with the band leader and asked him to interrupt the music for an announcement.

The band leader tapped on his glass and the room fell silent.

"This is an Amish dance!" he said. "This boy just left the Amish Community."

I had no idea what I was doing. I was rhythmically challenged but encouraged by the animated cheers and applauses I received.

"All those people," I thought to myself, "I wonder if they really are condemned to hell."

Although I doubted all the 'English' would burn in hell, I vowed I would eventually find out. Right now I just wanted to have some fun.

I asked Jim not to reveal my whereabouts to Dad because I did not want him to confront me. He agreed, understanding my plight.

My first night in the camper, I tossed and turned, reliving my escape and the exciting events that followed. Even though I had a long thorny path to follow, I felt the exhilaration of being a free man. It was a reprieve, a welcome liberation to be out of the shackles that kept me painfully chained to Dad, Church and the Amish Tradition.

Knowing I was a free man overpowered me. I wondered if I would be able to accept this reality and deal with the ramifications of being alone and on my own without a support system. However, the feeling of my unrestrained potential smothered any doubt or fear.

I rose form the bed and walked outside barefoot and bareheaded. The cool evening breeze caressed my hair. I was out of the darkness and in a magnificent world of color, music, animated voices and merriment; a world which would allow me to be anything I wanted and which encouraged me to become someone.

I was free to follow my own thoughts and dreams: I was free to live and exercise my right to make my own choices and decisions.

I thought of the baling wire whippings, the leather strap beatings, and the swift calloused, double hand slaps that caused so much pain and humiliation. It was all crammed into my yesterday. Today, however, I had a new reality. I would never again be whipped and condemned to hell by another man, just for living life as a free man.

Tears streamed down my face. For the first time in almost 21 years I wept for joy. There was no pain, no dishonor, no anguish or bleeding wounds. There was no grimacing face twisted in anger, no bitter resentments and no vindictive urges.

"God," I said, bowing my head, "thank you for giving me my freedom. I'm sorry for all the sins I've committed and hope you will forgive me. I promise to live my life with the hope of becoming a better person."

I felt relieved. Somehow I knew the Lord would help me achieve my goal. The choice was mine.

I felt a stirring in the pit of my stomach. It quickly swelled filling the icy void with a warmth I had never experienced before. Maybe it was love; maybe it was acceptance or perhaps it was finding a tiny bit of self-validation and dignity in the freedom I had just acquired. For the first time in my life I felt alive and couldn't wait for tomorrow. My thoughts were unlimited, my emotions were uninhibited and my actions were unhindered. I learned about the magnificence of hope and the joy of optimistic expectations.

It was 1993. I was almost twenty-one years old and at liberty to be me. I was physically, intellectually and spiritually free. More importantly, I was accountable only to God.

❋ ❋ ❋

Epilogue

I felt empowered in my newly acquired life as a 'modern' man and enjoyed the idea I could now control my own destiny, choose my own path and even worship the Lord in a manner that was congenial with my conscience. From the time I was a small boy in Bowling Green, Missouri, I had always coveted Dad's power until as a teen-ager I stood up for my dignity and self-respect and denied him the right to deliver physical punishments that were degrading and offensive. Although I had achieved a certain influence over him, I realized this was not the authority I needed for gratification. Unlike the power that dominates others, my new power allowed me the freedom to govern myself. Now my life belonged exclusively to me and I no longer had to be content with survival. I had the possibility to walk in any direction I wanted. There was nothing and no one with the power to stop me.

Although my journey would be an agonizing experience, mentally, physically and spiritually, I was certain my choices were justified. I was encouraged to continue. There would be no fear of retribution for errors and no guilt for enjoying a bit of life's pleasures. I traveled back in time, agonizing as it was to release all my buried torment, resentment and pain.

Liberated from the turmoil of my childhood and teen years

and purged of my bitter feelings, I feel empowered and eager to help others. Although the first part of my story ends here, my struggle to achieve autonomy, self-respect and dignity continued and brought me down many more dark and entangled roads before I was finally able to walk in the light. However, I hope my first book will be an inspiration to all who feel trapped in confining, abusive and humiliating situations. Man was born with free will and the right to a dignified existence.

Revealing the truth opened my mind, heart and soul. It gave me a special insight into the plight of the human being and more importantly it gave me the gifts of hope and faith. I do not fear the truth, though it is deeply painful. Instead, I will continue to speak the truth, relating my personal journey, until I am set free from my turbulent past. Today I know I can accomplish my purpose and be of assistance to others.

"You shall know the truth and the truth shall set you free!"

May you be blessed with the Lord's guidance, as I have been, and continue to be every day of your life.

Chris Burkholder